Edge of Wilderness

You are my Poems, Prayers and Songs

Joseph P. Shiel III

Aventine Press

Published by Aventine Press
55 East Emerson St.
Chula Vista CA, 91911
www.aventinepress.com

Library of Congress Control Number: 2012918162
Library of Congress Cataloging-in-Publication Data
Edge of Wilderness

ISBN: 1-59330-795-0

Contents

Booneville Hours

Dublin to Mayo

Steps in Time

A Heart's View

Dreams Afloat

You Are My …..

After the Falls

Love Sings

Tickles and Tastes

Acknowledgements

The meter was allowed to run, so to speak, for this creative endeavor into the wilderness, thanks largely to the following individuals who participated in the process and generously gave of their time, their efforts, their talents and inspiration to make the journey possible!

An abundance of thanks goes to Reverend Janet Nohavec for her determination, friendship, patience and loving, optimistic encouragement.

The great team of wonderful people at The Journey Within:

Patty Moran; for typing and outstanding deciphering of seemingly illegible chicken scratch,

Karen Rugar; for her patient PC skills and expertise and for bringing me into the twenty-first century

Jeffrey for his quick eye.

Tremendous thanks and appreciation belongs to Christine Buchanan; for her tireless organization, editing, decoding of the dyslexic mind and loving inspiration!

Robin; for her deep insight, true friendship, patient ear and musical enlightenment,

Gera; for challenging the depths of possibilities in healing,

Roger Corea; my mentor, for straight talk and real compassion,

Rick; for believing in me,

Deacon Mike and all the guys; for Faith Kentucky-style "No Problem",

My BC roommates; for competition, brotherhood and support.

Helen and Ken; for love and understanding,

The blessings that are my kids and entire family; for loving me anyway, despite the rollercoaster ride,

And finally, all my friends, too many to mention, you know who you are, for keeping me honest.

Dedication

There are so many moments of inspiration and love along the journey, through the Wilderness of the soul. I dedicate this book to all those who helped shape the path and challenge my steps.

To my children KT – Catherine, and Will – William;
For their continued love, inspiration and positively powerful efforts to change the world for the better.
I am so blessed to be their father.

In Memory
Of my mother Agnes, who passed at age thirty-nine when I was twelve.
She loved so that others might live to find joy.

In Memory
Of my Dad Joe, whose wisdom I miss greatly.
In a vision during a recent dream he approached me. I asked him, "What should I do about all the different things going on in my world"? He stated quite clearly, "Make a choice and then make another choice to be happy with the choice you've made."

Stansted Windows

The Old Man of the Lawn

Along the moss-strewn wall
Benches lay waiting, shading the wind-soaked leaves
Pinned and poised for assault
Thrust from the next northern gust
To the unexpecting, quiet fields beyond
Frozen in fear, only laid still by the frost of morning
Massive roots pierce and pull at the ground
As the barked arteries surround the heart of history.
Many eyes have known this king of the lawn
Who holds their stares as he stretches his hands to heaven
Shadows of dark, twist and turn, interwoven
Framing the vast brilliant blue
Of the outer edge of God's viewing case
"Watch me" cries the king
For the time has come to lead again.
Hallowed figures dressed and saying grace
The weathered benches applauding silently
The massive majesty then joins the shout of generals
Across the great manor
And the wind of their voices cracks the glass sleeves of morning's chill
That glistens on the arms and fingers of the old man
The strong muscular reaches that have held up heaven so long
Begin to wave the flags to spirit's cheers
The clashes of vibrations against the still dawn's air
Snap and pound the drums of the regiment
The slaps and cracks of experienced wood against time
Sound the attack
And the dead leaves awake below the wall
As they leap for the attack, for freedom, for more
Into the patient fields that long to catch the fire of change

Anthony's Feet

The pebbles shift and crinkle
Below the thrust of the runner's feet
The wee little man flies by and touches down stride for stride
Like a stone skipping across a quiet pond
He whisks with energy
To break the quiet of the dawn
His thoughts awake with the shadowy giants
At the far reaches of the fields
And as he glides crackling the grass, frozen below the frost
He will not yield
He won't believe we've lost
The heart of a giant angel
With wings of thought to fly
The rhythm of each leap defies all death
We never die
As woven as the branches in the royal, stately trees
His thoughts never quiet and collide in each new breeze
Filled with wonder and fierce against the holes and ditches
That threatens the runner's path
He springs ever forward
He stretches his reach
He runs like a white-tail buck
He won't allow the wrath
As swift as an eagle
As smooth as a dolphin's fin
He challenges the darkness and brings the morning in
He runs upon the clouds of dew
And spreads a wake against the fog
He brings so much to this suffering earth
And yet he just calls it
A simple Jog

The Blossoms of Spring

The blossoms of spring
Dance upon the limbs of the magnolias
As the brisk breeze is chatting and sweeping
It swings and sways as I pass by
Blessing hands of the youthful tree
Appear like a gypsy along the road
Casting spells against the cold
"Give me a few more minutes"
She seems to wisp and shout
Before the setting sun
Her colors illuminate
Licking-up what's left of the burning sky
She summons in the summer land
For she casts spells
Against the cold heart of winter's harsh final stand
She thrashes at the gust of evening
Apparently worried about a frost
Screaming, "I will not die… All is alive and lives"
The spring is never lost

Great Steed

O stand quiet
Great steed
Painting your majestic landscape
Across the greenery of the old lawn
The weight of your hooves holding
The spinning earth at stillness
Your powerful four pillars
Straight and sturdy as your muscular back
Holds up the sky
What nobler stance
Of attention could you
Pose
      Stillness
        Quiet
          Strength
         And
          Repose

You are more than a rider's dream
You are God's hope
   The picture
     Of peace

Heaven's Window

Each soul
Like the fractal figure of a dewdrop iced alive
Etched like fine crystal
Frozen to the glass pane just at the tip of my nose
Through the old weathered frame, the secret windows of heaven
Each mansion, every room
A magical yet necessary luminary
Adding form, shape, texture, musical symmetry
To a multi-faceted prism, interlocked with millions
Reflecting and shedding the dance of light
Sparkling and delicate
Glistening and strong
Brilliantly salt and peppered
Distilling a diverse storm of colors
Rainbowed before the day
Each shine and shimmer, embracing arm in arm
Life aloft on the stillness and silence of the bitter cold
They warm the heart of love within
Defining my tiny existence
Radiating my brilliant significance
For beauty always remains, forever after
Even behind the cloudiest skies
Through the darkest most frigid eve
All will be for goodness sake
The morning star has melted their purpose
Has blinded the truth of immeasurable creation
And birthed another challenge
To squint, to search, to struggle, to catch a glimpse
To hope, to see
Through some lonely window
A drop of God
Rains through like a king

The Mantle of Greatness

Workmanship still stands adorning
The cornice of the windows and door
"Live on" carpenters, plaster men
Artisan of then.
Some say art is objective, of no value
That it means nothing in the end
That it's not necessary,
Can't feed your belly, shelter your kin
How short sighted, shallow and stale
Can greedy fools be
Where is their intelligence,
Why is it they can't see
Arts and crafts are all about
In everything we know
All that is conceived or made
In all the firsts we sew.
The style of a dwelling
The function of this pen
Without the art and artisan
We become Neanderthals again.
Art is of inspiration, invention and the soul
And valued by the intelligent
Because without it
The world won't grow

Tea Room

Jet streams plaid the morning sky
Dissipating to disguise themselves as clouds
Innocently awash behind the shadowy textures
Of the masterful tree lines
At the far end of the great green
The grove stands still, hushed
Umbrellaing the distant stone walls
Still damp from the evening's dreams
They meditate, prostrated
With the weight of heavy dew
Before her majesty the college
Each tree still, steadfast, alive and strong
Patient and poised to meet the day
Like royal guard across the lawn
Speechless and yet loudly powerful
To hold the gate
And protect the gape
Of Arthur's holy gifts
Sing, birds of morning and rejoice
Although many may not have the means
To enter her womb of knowledge
The world will receive the new life
Her minds will bring

Roses

The wind whips the trees to wave hello
As the roses on the old trellis dance below
So many dancers young and old
Some bright, strong and open
To embrace the midday sun
Others withered petals, crippled and weak
Dropping their feathers, carpeting beneath wandering feet
They still rise from the garden
In a ballerina's poised pose.
As the wind gusts again and the waltz begins
Could I let go of my roots and loosen hold of my vines?
Let the breeze carry me and dance with them free for a time
To feel beautiful, fragrant, masterful and sweet
To lay open myself
To wash a wanderers feet.

My own trellis has broken many times in its day
But the garden of dancers within my heart stay
My colorful companions and vibrant new seed
Bring the music of songbirds and whispers through trees
So let my roses dance
I offer my petals to soften your race to a stroll
For if I don't dance with the roses
I may never feel my soul

Sunday Morning

O Sunday morning
The day of rest
SABBATH
Dear God, if only I could
Dear God to rest
To quiet my mind
Put aside my thoughts
Of fears, past years
And shortened tomorrows

To ease away the inner panting and ranting
Of pain and disillusionment
To embrace the stillness
For a few moments
Catch a breath of light

Dear God, sit close to me
Hold my stillness
A moment of peace
My troubles are but simple lessons
Sign-posts, pathways, detours
To align me to your side
To want the Sabbath
The Sunday morning
The quiet love
That my heart has known with you
Sit, let me hold you
And wipe away
Your fears

The Orchestra

The garden stands like an orchestra just to the side of the presence
Of the stately and appointed brick, towering, corbelled chimneys
And vast glass windows
Orderly and at attention
Watching the gentle pull
Of the massive lawn, draped like a beard
Pressed beneath the jaw of her foundation
The landscape makes love to her
As the breezes gently move the muscular arms of giant trees
Into a hug to caress her frame
The orchestra stirs in excitement as if tuning-up for a celebration
Their colors melt before the sun and their instruments sing out to the
morning
"There is love"
Oh, holy are you my Stansted queen
She stands reverent and beautiful
Beneath the cotton-flowered spring bonnet of sky
Her face radiant in love with her charge
She stands timeless, aware of her admirers
And committed to heal upon welcome
Her hand of peace stretched across the sidewalks, gardens and lawns
She cradles every new seeker and smiles deep into their gaze
Oh, how I love to adore her charm and grace
How blessed we are
To waltz into this place

Magpie

Oh, magpie how your tuxedo fits
As you sit and dance upon the branch
Of a sapling at the edge of the majestic, manicured greens
Like the mâitre d'
You greet the morning, feathering about busy as a bee
Determined in your pose
Without your presence the day would stand still
The morning would not awake
So I am glad you dressed
And watched over the garden
Scanning the great manor's lawn
For you are morning, my tuxedo friend
You stand at England's dawn

A Spot of Green Tarnish

A spot of green tarnish stares back at me
From the base of the entry hall chandelier
Which lights the great stages of stairs
Marked by cathedral newel posts, spiking their way to heaven
The spot seems to know me, we have obviously met before
An image of a man immersed in the century's old mansion looks on
Victorian furnishings are wrapped in velvet maroon
And swell to even greater girth by the ball of the brass
Lost in a spray of faces, smiling
In deep discussion from days gone by
And yet alive in the hollows of this foyer
The giant wall containing the history
The stature, the knowledge, the hope
All swell to greater shimmer

Behind the tarnish of the world
There is bright reflection

Arthur Findlay's Grave

A hint of a grey stone
Sturdy, intact yet so old
One must stretch their minds
To imagine her dedication
Long before she was somewhat hidden
By the girth of greenery
Held by the heavy elephant-skinned
Oaks, hickories and such
Still considered virgins in their day
Although it would not be a first thought
Upon greeting their aged, drooping, massive limbs
Beaten and shaped
Weathered by time
Her stained jewels
Ornately sculpted,
Peek through the brush of a spring morning
As she reaches to catch her sun
In the distance
Majestic, yet as powerful
As a cathedral castle
Tall, she stands
The little church is surrounded
By a moat of floating souls
Aswim among the headstones
Of believers
Hugging her foundation and reaching out
In some corners, ten deep
Flanking her perimeter
Weary from the war of waiting
A regiment of loyal, faithful warriors
Guarding her skirt and yet
Riding her apron
In hopes of more
In anticipation of safety, security
Of continuance

Of the possibility of
Heavenly reward.
And at last there is one among them
Who lives his truth and will not die
If only we could brave her ancient frame
And say, "Rest me lady"
Thank you for your prayers
We will always surround your quiet song
And breathe with continuous life

Birds Afloat

Upon the fresh spring wind
The voices announce the morning
The chill breaks the skin
And daylight brings violet luster
Framing the gentlemen of the lawn
Green blankets, of fine mist
Rest upon earth
Quiet pierces the space and time
Of the ceiling's height.
Blue room accented by the clicks
And sweeping clacks
Of a clock spinning under glass
Atop the modest mantel
It is this time now, and now again
The moment when love is possible
The breath of now
The peace of morning
The anticipation and surrender
Of life's air, of a heart's truth
Of me, to quiet possibilities, peace
Surely emerging from the dark space
This sleep

God's Wings

The grand ole tulip trees sweep and dip
And puff their wings against the morning
Angels awaken tall
Warrior protectors
Watching over the dawn
Angels of quiet, patient busy-ness
Waiting for just the right moment
That perfect unnoticed time
To attack the dark and dreary night
To hurl themselves upon the depression of winter
To strike out with magnificent fury
And lay waste to doubt and fear
To blossom for beauty's birth
To conquer questions of truth
To capture the runners
To rescue angels home
The tulip tree in bloom
Holds God's wings around you

Wings of Hope

Joined Again – A Prayer for Jack

Allow me one more moment, although it is not enough
To recall, recap and recover
Reason, relations and regard
Allot me one brief instance, align me with your least
Touch me with the truth
Rain on me garments of light
Although I have wandered
All the moments of my thoughts
Teach me
Still
Your plan for me, raise me by your hand
Alleviate me from my evils
Alert my arms to embrace your love
Remove the walls I have placed between us
Feed me
To your deepest need
Allow me one more moment, alone I am not enough
To romance, relive and recover
Reality, responsibility, root
Allot me no more breaths
Alive
My life turned toward you
Take me on a walk with those we love
Bury me in your purpose for all
For all is so quick and quiet now
A loud rush
I trust the fire of your peace
Torch my very being
Enflame my lonely heart
Weld me to your spirit
My love, my Lord
Allow me one moment
Before I come home

I Know Some Angels

I know there are some angels
I've seen some here and there
Holding other's burdens
Sharing, carrying things they couldn't bear

I know there are some angels
Not winged, like picture books
But plain... simple... tall... and short
Plain folk... straight talk... peaceful looks

I know there are some angels
A handful, even more
They keep appearing in my life... in my heart
Somehow unlocking the doors

I'm sure! There are true angels!
I know now they don't work alone
Strangers maybe, family, friends
But their hearts call Heaven their home

It's true! There are some angels!
I'm so grateful that they're real
They took my stale and hollowed heart
And made it full... and feel

Angels by the Window

An angel stood outside my window smiling bright through the night
The angel stood by the old woman's window waiting to provide
Curtains wave in a gentle breeze
As the old woman's fragile eyes can't see
The night sky opens, the stars shine bright
It was time to lead her through the night

The angels gathered with songs of joy
For a life lived hard, was no more

Welcome home my love
We want you to be at peace above
Welcome home my love

The angel stands beside every window
By the side, to lead them home
The angel smiles at every window
To let us know we are not alone

The Soul Is My Most Precious Creation

The soul,
Like the roses of my garden
The favorite joy of my heaven
Each unique and yet
Blindingly similar in its growth,
They must be like seeds sown into the
Fabric of existence, nurtured and challenged
So that they struggle
To reach maturity, beauty and birth
The soul brings from its conception
My truths into awareness

Rich with information, each individual soul
Will conform and adjust
To align its own experience
For the greater good, maturity of the whole planet
Growth of each is interdependent upon the other
For the health
And well-being of the world

New seeds will be spread across my garden
They will feel at times, similar
Knowing there is no such thing as a soul mate
Only soul familiarity, one to another
A family, a color in the spectrum
Of the greater beauty of my garden

Souls thrive and survive their journey to maturity
To complete surrender, to a concern for all others
To flower fully before the sunlight
Of my undying Love
Who am I, you might ask?
Who determines the soul?
I am that I am
The gardener

The first Seed
The one who permeates
And is ever present in each
I am responsible for your flower
As you are equally responsible for mine
You are all me, all mine.
Love each other and flower
Do not falter
Or fade

A Letter to God

You are a friend
I didn't know you were a friend
Then again, I didn't know I didn't know
You were a friend
What's a friend?
I didn't know what a friend was

Then again I didn't know
I didn't know
You were a friend
Oh, I thought I knew, I know I thought I knew
But no, no buts

Denial as it goes you know
Acceptance as it is or will be
Your will be – not mine
Because I know, I know I didn't know
I know now I don't, and when I do, your will, will be done

A Little Voice

This morning I heard a voice call out
It seemed to come from far above
The dawning of a beautiful new world
Would rise from the least amongst us
With an awesome power of love

In a place long forgotten
Hundreds of years behind the dreams
There would be a new light of creation
The sound of children laughing
Instead of the fears, tears, and silent screams

Far from the stone of the pilgrims landing
Far from freedom's mansioned shores
Through the sticky heat and dusty bush mud huts
A new rock is placed as a foundation
To build a holy respect for life once more

So gather round this festive table
There are only stories of what once was lost
A grateful child became a beacon
A whole new world has grown to illuminate the truth
And change the hearts of nations, no matter what the cost

A Thanksgiving voice ascends upon the earth today
From the heavens of many mansions above
There begins a vision of a new creation
Where children are allowed to dream
A world builds with the hands of love

No more suffering bodies
No more hungry minds
No more broken spirits
No more thirsty hearts
No more… "The kid's not mine"

Could You Show Me

Could you show me a different plane
Some place that's just not the same
A place where there may never be suffering and pain
Can you show me a better place
One I can see with my own face
Where there is a better time for this human race
Will you show me to the sky
A heaven I can see with my own eyes
Where there is no hate or poverty, a place where we can see why
Can you lead me to a hill, where I can see war go still
And no one will ever wish to kill.
Oh, can your angels show the way
To a better time, a better day
Oh, can your spirit teach us, Lord
That we can be healed and love
Where there is no fear in God

Walls

You knocked upon my door
I answered only walls
You called me out by name
But I refused the call

You whispered through a window
In fear I drew the shade
You shouted from the roof tops
I was angry and enraged

I lived inside these walls
I built them hard and strong
I've reveled in the workmanship
That left me safely from the storms

I've watched others let you in
But they were weak and frail
I told myself, I'm not like them
I must build my walls of steel

My walls became too many
I had built myself a maze
I became trapped and lonely
Desperate to be saved

You knocked upon my door
I ignored your gentle plea
The walls came crashing down
And knocked me to my knees
I opened the door slightly
You rushed in like the day

You charged in like the light
Forgave me for the stall
You held me like a child
And raised me up so tall

You cleared away my path
Gave me steps that I might climb
You carried my heavy past
And healed my wounds with time

And now the walls have been opened
My things have been put away
My life is no longer broken
Since Jesus came to stay

Job for the Day, God

You take one side
I'll take the other
And together we can lift
The Spirit of hope for
A friend
A brother
A sister
Who is lame to faith
Disillusioned with life
Broken by disappointment
Alone to wandering
Hungry or cold
Young or frail
Lost and confused.
You take one side, God
I'll take the other
Together we can lift them,
Lift them to see
Your face
In the mirror
Of my soul

Angel's Wing

There's a place above the earth for all of us
There's a place where we can find peace
I won't hold you back
I will love you there forever, it will last

There's a place where angels dwell on high
There's a place where angels always find their way back home
I will take you there
Above all the world
In a place of dreams of every boy and girl

There's a place where poverty doesn't exist
There's a place where everyone loves each other first
I'm going to find my way back home again
I'm going to take you by the hand and show you where it all began
A whole new song
That's where you've all begun and where you belong

It's not so far away, it's in your mind
It's there for everyone, and it's finally the time
Come hear my song
My poem and my words
Finally find our way back home
It's not so hard to understand what's going on
It's all in a larger plan to be found
So please see the light of all that is right
Know that I love you for all of your life

You'll find a place on high
A place where you never die
You'll find a place above all the pain and strife
Take an angel by the wings
Hear them as they sing
For love is what they bring

The Mission

I've lived my life from a sense of greed
I've found myself losing my values to a sea of pain
I carried all the weight of bleeding shame

What did you do boy
What is that I hear
What are you calling me to do
What is it that I fear

I carry the baubles and trinkets of my life
Carry the brokenness of all the strife
I've broken hearts and I've broken many men
Been so far lost I didn't know where to begin

What is that you say
What is that you do
Where will I find my hope
Where will I find my truth

I will climb the mountain
That rises to the skies
And drop the pain like teardrops from my eyes

I am yours
I am all yours ....now
I will rejoice with you
I will kneel down on the mountain
And you will show me the way through
I have no need left for me
I drop everything to my knees
My heart is finally soaring free
For thee

Wind Against the Snow

Is that the wind against the snow
Or is it angel's wings aglow
So long my heart has been so cold
Lord knows I could use an angel right now

I can't believe all I received this morning
I didn't think that it was time
I didn't even know how I would respond
Behind all of my pride.

Is that the wind I hear at my window
There is something so near I can taste it
Is that an angel or is that you my love
Why can't I see you
Why can't you think of me, my love
Oh what a morning, oh how hard
Why don't they give fair warning
For the shattering of a heart.

Is that the wind I feel on the back of my neck
Or is that you drawing near
Who can tell me
Can it be true
Could it be
Can an angel finally bring you to me

I don't know what words to use
Who can tell me
Can it be true, could it be
Did an angel finally bring me to you

I don't know what words to use
How do you tell someone, you love them so
How do you say a word between the pain
Is that the wind just blowing in the snow

Was that your angel carrying you

Each flake I see is whispering prayers to me
Full heart, it can't be true
I hope the angels have you safe in their arms
I hope they carry you as high as can be
I hope the gate is wide open, love
Would you hold it open for me

Someday the snow will come again
It will drift past my door
Whispering love, we'll be together once more

Angels carry you home
Angels carry you
Wait for me

Someday

I will be the brilliant white gloss
Streaking across a leaf
Reflecting and refracting the sun
Light and movement
An aid to illuminate the morning

Someday
I will be a pebble on the garden walk
Laying quietly among the thousands
Holding the warmth close to mother's skin
And as others step through the day
I will get to help carry the weight of life's journey

Someday
I will be a single droplet
Of mysterious dew on the lawn
Allowed to float and hover
And melt into the morning's view

Someday
I will be a gust of wind
A breeze tickling through the petals of daffodils
Awakening them to the sky
And opening their hearts
To entice the pollination of more

Someday
I will be the sweet symphony
Of vibrations of a bee's wings
Sounding the call of dance
Breaking the silence
And stirring the call to live

Someday
I will be a moss-covered stone
Among the strong rocks of the long field wall

Steadfast, sturdy, defining the land
Following a true path
Holding the line of distance and time

Someday
I will be a stretch of thick bark
Along a low sweeping branch
Of a grand old Tulip tree
Bending and adapting my reach
From the depths of shade
To pure blue sky

Someday
I will be a molded red brick
Mortared into a massive wall
Of a college manor
Holding up history
Weathering centuries of heaven's tears

Someday
I will be the quiet
Through the high ceiling halls
Embracing the hand-carved woodwork
Adorned with the marbled mantels
In the still of the silence
As knowledge waits for so many

Someday
I will be the tock following the tick
Of a fine clock on the wall
Behind the sound of beginning
Drowned out by discussion
Philosophizing and laughter
Confused by clinking plates
And teacups at breakfast
And tolling the end of each moment
To effort forward

Someday
I will be one and many things
Enticing with all the senses I can muster
To reach the reaches of all intelligences
To know one and all
And all as one

Someday
I will be a blade of grass
On the manicured lawn
Significant in color, form, position and time

Someday
I will be purpose
I will be one
I will truly be love

Someday
Some hour
Some moment
Perhaps right now
Someday

One Day

One day there will be a sky that flows above the peace
One day there will be a place safe for you and me
I see a world full of all that is good
A place that is kind and caring of each and everyone

There is no more war
No more pain
No more lost children
They're all loved all the same
Everyone can find a meal or a shelter for rest
Love and patience from the elders
That can explain all the reasons why
A world where we honor each other's most holy place
A world where we finally see God's wonderful face

I'm not speaking of a world of golden robes and giant gates
I'm not speaking of a world where we are floating
In some imaginary place
I'm not speaking of a world that just can't be
I'm speaking of a world where I can see all of us free

It's not difficult or hard to understand
I'm speaking of a world of a fellowship of man
It's not so confusing or impossible you see
It's a world where we help each other
Where we love each other free

Sometime today look into a child's face
Try to see the whole world as a much different place
Not one that tears down our brother and your sister's hearts
Not one that compares each other just to tear each other apart

I speak of a world that is not impossible to reach
I speak to you now from all that I can see
From ocean to ocean
From beach to beach
From all the mountain tops that we could reach
From every inlet, polar cap to cap
This is what we need, it can happen in a snap
All we need is to journey inside
Bring out the things that we all hide
Turn then to the souls above
See the grace of God's love
You see, all it takes is love
All it takes is love

As I Live and Breathe

Dad always said, "It's a cinch by the inch, a trial by the mile".
There are many miles for people like me, before I grow weak enough
Frail enough and blind enough to appreciate the inch
There, the trial finds me
There, I throw myself at the mercy of love
There, I cinch it
For miles I have come and yet miles wait, so I choose the inch

Love =Truth=God

In the beginning
As in the end
There is only love
Which, is the Truth
Anything less than Love
Is simply
Not of Truth
Not Of God

The Spark of Thought

With every thought
We move the moment
With every heart
We move the soul

If we are apart
We will become broken
As we come together
We come to truly know

In every moment, energy will flash and shine
In every loving thought you will know the Divine
In every heart there can be true light

Beyond the pain, blindness and darkened voices
Of the soul's own fears
Your love brings the kindness
That frees joyful tears

Booneville Hours

Sick and Tired

There is so much noise
In the silence of my evening
A thunder of fear
A storm of past storms
Into the quiet like a dark wood
The sounds unseen startle my spirit
Visions of lightning bolts
Drenched in a rain of sweat
Salted for the feast
For I am the meal of my own horrors
To be served up well-done
Hardened and charred by the burning flames
Of hopes, dreams, aspirations
Only to be basted with the slick, spicy booze
Which drips quickly off my brain
And caramelizes around my feet
Holding me stuck, out of balance
And exposed in the middle of all
Leered at, jeered at, laughed at, pitied
Gawked at, spewed at, jabbing at my heart
What I would give for a drink
To melt my thirst to try
What I wouldn't do for a cooler
For other losers and simple minds of consequences
Some man of God I've become
Preaching - Believe
And hearing only - Leave
For I'm worthless, a screw-up, toast and jam
Lost, lonely, dangerous and a waste
So much noise
I am sick and tired, God
Obviously my pain is my own
I guess I should pick up the phone

Tools of My Heart

My mind begins the crinkling
Of its morning connection
Catching memories and feelings
Of yesterday's experiences
Recapturing yet another
Precious day
Aside and behind
Put to storage, for what?
Like a hoarder's room
Stacked with old papers

Lord, help me to awaken
To turn on the overhead lights
Illuminating the accumulation
Of fears, wasted moments, distracted thoughts
Emotional strains, repeated, restless regrets

Help me, Lord, to grab them up
Realize their uselessness
In the great creative hall of my being
Give me strength
To see through them
From the windows of my soul
Into the lineage of time
Allow me only now, empty, stripped of my chains
My uniforms, my costume
Left hungry, open, willing
For a more cherished breath of hope
God, you allow me so much room
To create something new, better, significant
With the tools of my heart

Whatever

Whatever you fear
Leave it in the arms
Of the Lord
Whatever shudders, shakes
And shatters
The shell of your soul
Let the sun and the sand
Soothe the harsh
Slivers of your heart
Let the ocean waves of love
Wash over you from above
And heal the heart's horror
And harried thoughts
Pour the salt of the sea
Into the wounds of yesterday
And let your mind swim
To the horizon of better dreams
Choose to ride the wind
To skip over the water
To fly free
Before the sky
Leave your fears
In the arms
Of the world

For in love is to live
Fear is to die

There's Always Hope

There's always hope inside of love
There's no room for great inside of love
I will show you how much it means

There's no room for pain inside of love
There's no room for failure inside of love

I will show you love
I will bring you there
There's no one greater
No one lesser in love
No one hiding behind the clouds above
It's all right here, it's always been
You're the one to hold the magic within
I will show you how
I will show you all within love
I will give you all my love

There's no room for brokenness
No such thing as pain and fear
No such thing as weakness in love
It's all right there to be seen
You can find it in the quiet now
It's not like you're making the scene
It's there anyhow and always has been

There's no hatred or pain in love
And everyone is connected
You and me and all there is
It's only a matter of time now
Till we come to peace
It's only a matter of words and thoughts
It's what I'm ready to see

Think of Your Journey

Think of your Journey
How simple is the day with God
Shallow muddy rivers
Rock faces
Steep trails
Shadow sunrise
Straight, tall oaks and cedars
Climb to blue
Puff clouds, soaring hawks
Fly over cathedral cliffs
Chasms dip, tiers of tears
Fall to deep caves
And darkened rapids below
Smooth weathered walls
Feathered tall grass
Winding mountain roads
Rocks jagged, covered with
Colors of green, ivy, yellow
Fire red, brushed blue clay
Split rail stairway ascension
Wild flowers, fresh air
Alive

Chattered talk
Laughter on the walk
Ivy figures and rich green moss
Mushrooms nestled between the roots
Leaves crackling beneath our boots

Wander and wonder and wind on in
God's good earth
Struggle with reason and purpose
Since the day of my birth

Died in Him
And Risen with His name
The Journey continues
My will, my pain

Swimming holes and barn poles
Tobacco sheds, black ash
The coal mine just up ahead
Corn fields and fences
Clothes lines in the shade
Quite an awesome picture
He's made
Quite a simple day
Wouldn't you say?
Set a spell, take it in

I Thought of the 100 Arches Today

I thought of the 100 Arches
Again
Nature's bridges across
Rugged terrain
And troubled waters
With a view of Heaven
Awesome and powerful
Bridging the gap of mountain tops
Cathedral cliffs
And wild, untamed
Dangerously treacherous roads
The ones less traveled

I thought of us building
Together in these mountains
Searching for the
Natural bridges

I thought for a minute
Of our connections
Our hilltops
And balconies
Our offices and comforts
Our cathedrals
Full parking lots on Sunday
Our families
Home

So Slow It Goes

So slow it goes, the materials, the trash, the rotting floor
No water, no bathroom
Loaded shot guns, barking dogs

The ad reads;
Quiet 2 bedroom home on two acres
Park-like setting
On a private, elegant crushed stone drive
With privacy gate
Complete with antiques
And a view of the mountains
Low electric
Virtually no water, utilities
Or cable on site
Minutes to anywhere, only 20 minute commute
To the largest town in the county
Open, airy construction
Early American décor
A wealth of possibilities
A must see!!
For appointment call Pielher Realty 1-800-Holler Christ
I am kidding, of course, but we are asked to build bridges.

Dear Lord
I ask only that I may know
The drafty windows in my life
The things I haven't finished
Where I have left myself
And my family open to the cold
And the winds of evil

That I may see the trash
I leave outside my door
The trash I have yet to take
Responsibility for

Those things I refuse or deny
To correct or pick up after
For fear of being pegged
With my ownership
Of them

I pray I may see
The sparseness in my own home
Where my cupboards are bare
Bare of the food of God
The moments wasted, piled outside
The nourishing spirit of practiced prayer
And the host of words of encouragement
Devoured on Sundays
And left barren for weeks on end

I beg to recognize
My own distance from the center of Christ
My isolation from my own truth
My loaded shotguns
My fences in thought
My refusal to change
The rituals of my hypocrisy
To venture out with an open mind
And a willing heart

I wonder about my own
Powerlessness
Those situations
Relationships, things
That have become unmanageable
In my life

Where do I turn,
How long do I wait?
Do I blame, accuse, rage
Or do I commune with
And trust In God's love for me?
Do I reach to my brothers,
To my God?
Do I raise a finger
From the steering wheel of my life
To greet the heart of my fellows
Or drive on by?

Today, I will think of poverty
Not of the physical realities all about,
But of the reality
Of the condition
Of the Trailers
Of my own soul

Let's go build bridges

Listen to the Rain

Shhhhhhhh
Listen to the whisper
Of the rain
Listen to the syncopated
Rhythms of the sloppy,
Rocky mud beneath
My boots
Hear the hint of a full day
And the pleasing
Grunts and groans of
The men

Listen to the whisper
Of the rain
Hear the joy
Of the Lord
In the day's pleasant pain
Listen to the whisper of the rain
Shouting light to come again

Stung By a Bee

Stung by a bee
Floating like a butterfly
Down for the count
Praying not to die

In the middle of nowhere
Deep in the woods
Ginseng and squirrel hunting
Far from store goods

Side-winders, copperheads
Rattlers you see
And I'm taken out by
By a little ole bee

A Light Rain

A light rain sprawls itself over
The green blanket of the holler
Dragging down the morning fog
To rest upon the tobacco beds

Again I find myself
Winding down the blue grass mountains
Stumbling into prayer
Watching the mortar of my walls
Crack and shatter
The whisper says
"Let go, let the Lord work"

A light rain sprawls itself over
The flesh of my face
Dragging down the blanket of fears
To rest upon the bed of my heart
They gently rustle in the breeze of my soul
Shaped by God's hands
The edges smooth to a soft roll
Like the hills so abundantly
Given me in the blessings
Of Kentucky

Kentucky Mountains

Partial light burning through
The fog of dawn
A soft, warm
Wash of color
Rising from the embers
Of morning
Behind sleeping mountains

The mist of my dreams
Slowly melts away
As the morning prayers
Burn and sizzle
The dew on my soul

The rhythm of voices
And tones of heavens unknown
Sneak over the mountains of my life
There they stream into
The hollows of my heart.
Pierced by light, I recognize
My broken, Jagged truths
And melt in the calm, serene quest
Of the brilliant sun
Shining over the peaks of the
Kentucky Mountains

I thank you Lord

Lucky

There once was a young man
From Kentucky
Who was considered by some
Rather Lucky

The story travels
Fast you see
About this man named Robert Creech
And his Poplar trees

It seems way back in his holler
At the end of the road
Robert wanted to build a house
And call it a home

But a quaint mountain cabin
Or humble abode
Began to grow to the size
Of the Astrodome

He cut trees to make the building lot
Then he milled some lumber
So it wouldn't be bought
But it wasn't nearly enough
Not even close

"I have more trees"
Robert was heard to boast
So he cut more trees
Then more and more
But it still wasn't enough
For windows or doors

So he cut still more
And had them hauled to the mill
God help him finish this house
If it be your will

Somewhere in Kentucky
You can hear trees fall
As a house grows wider
Longer and tall

Saws scream rough lumber
Wet with bark
Dear God we'll be building in
The dark

"Enough already, Robert"
I heard yelled
As I heard yet another
Tree as it fell

"Please stop" I thought,
Enough
The mountain is bald
And the house is as big
As the East View Mall

So goes the story of
Robert Creech
Who would tell you himself
That building
Is no day at the beach!!

Cathedral Mountains

Gentle breezes sweep and whirl
Licking the lips
Of the taller leaves,
They whistle and wave as tall poplars sway
Oceans of blue
Kissed peacefully by puff clouds
Rest upon their quiet crest
Like steep cathedrals
Watching over my dreams
That wander a fond caress

Pleasant pain and tired aches
Stiffen my pace
While the aroma of the animals
Mixes and twists
Amidst fried chicken and the
Mortar on my fingertips

My God, my Jesus is released
And pleased
As again and again I'm driven to my knees
A warm day's work of donuts
And laughter

Sweet dreams roll over me
Cool my burning heart
Quiet rhythm of swaying
Cheering on blue skies
Deepen my gaze
Inside my shaken soul
Steep cathedral mountains
Embrace me
And squeeze out my fears

Pleasant pain and tired aches
Stirring me to life
Sweet and sour smells
Of the rich dark earth
Weep through my tears
And pierce the center of my armor.
As I kneel to place the corner stone
Of this blessed home,
I feel your chiseling upon me
Shaping the sanity,
The mortar of my soul
Building me anew
Framing my heart to stand strong

Dear Lord

Tear me apart
Rip me into jagged pieces
Cut me into a pile of ribbons
Slice me to a pathetic mess

Grab me and choke out the truth
Squeeze me to a desperate dying breath
Scatter my hollowed heart across the crowd
Grind me to a steaming mulch

Beat me senseless to a simple word
Taunt my trilogy to confused compliance
Heave me high and drop me hard to my knees
Gauge my sight to a brief vision

Shout so loud so I hear only the silence
Sour my thirst to sweet surrender
Run me to a crawl
Place me at such a distance that I can do nothing but want

Toss me so alone and so shattered that I'm willing to do anything
Use all my time if you must
If only for one shocked moment I recognize you
Wrench my being to expose my brokenness
Contort my purpose and enslave my will to yours

Show me vividly, my fears and crush my past
Throw scandal in my path and confine me to today
Play me like a fiddle so I feel the music
Paint me as the landscape open to the hawk

Cast me in your play, if only a minor role
Declare a war on me for peace
Hold me as you love me
And waltz me to your dance …..Serenity

Dublin to Mayo

Weathered Shoals

Roll in and lift the feathers atop your many faces
As you roar in from some distant edge of earth
Preaching your power, line after line in formation
Waving a spray of greetings
Grabbing at every moment with a splash of rhythms
You nod and curl back
Threatening your temporary stay
Teasing and tickling the flesh
Of my freezing tufts of hair
Amidst the peaks and valleys of my weathered shoals
Mere wrinkles of aged memories
Browned by the heat of changes
And grayed white by the cold
Of drifting, scouring sands of glassy dreams
You sparkle and move mysteriously
Rich in the cobalt of your deep blues
You shine like a cathedral window
Demanding my attention, begging my eyes
To dance in the light, away from the shadows
Of the mortared walls and bolted pews
Encouraged by the vast infinite swells
Reaching for possibilities of love and peace
In the sands of our times
I hear the screams of the winds
The howl of the storm
And gentle whispers of the breezes
As yet another burst of consistency, strength and beauty
Crashes against my beach
And smoothes the prints of pain
I embrace your horizon
With each wet kiss of your salty scent
And I melt beneath you

Ireland
Heritage - Thoughts for My Son

Rise ye sweeping stone mountains
Wrapped in heather, pine and hay
Sharp you pose against a clouded sky
Shaped ye are before the silver sea
Guiding the river long in from the ocean
Gilded with the finest of fish
The brave darn their vest and bamboo rod
Then set a dory to the valley pond
Pines and cedars peak out from the hills
Pipers of old are heard in the evergreen breeze of evening
Birds sing a final song, summoning home
Broken as my heart may be
T'is dear Delphi that soothes the soul
The mountains and hills of Mayo
Won't leave your heart alone

There's Something About Joes

There is something about Joes
Something that lasts
That sits on the mind from time to time
Perhaps it's familiar, or just easy to remember
There's a toughness to the nature
You can call on Joe, you know

Then the one you can sit down with
For an old cup-a-Joe
That whole bible thing can't be ignored
Joseph with tenderness, vulnerable to the world
Yet patient, kind, quiet, reserved
The father in the background of morning
At work throughout the day
Learning still, so much to say

Joey as a boy at times, to lighten the air
Joseph at other times, if he ever so dared
With Josephs it's fathers, sirs and dads
There is always the wonder
Of the thoughts sons had
To watch a man always struggle
Yet always a step ahead of your own
Attention to every detail, some now that you own

So much was said and unsaid
To some, was to be or not to be
It's true for a father
Life lived to the best that he can
Can only lead a son to be even a greater man

So Joe and Joseph by any and many a name
Sir, the memories were enriching
Every time they came
No matter what Joseph's life span
No matter how he lived the game
My son
Joe loved ya
Just the same!

Quiet Dock

The long, ribbed lap of a Dory
Lay aside a quiet dock
Lopping and lapping up a few sips
Of a rippled wind-kissed sky
As the browns and greens, tans
And yellows spread themselves
Across the gloss between the currents
And are only pricked by an occasional slap
Of the more clever fish,
Warrior tails,
Who survived another day
Of the long boats and the infantry
Along the banks of the valley bath
Mounds of strength, grace and color
Life from the timeless tale
Move before the sun
And stacks of pillowed clouds.
She lays quiet and soaks my stare
Her boney cap poised to awake
Her muscular thighs lifting the floating forest
Summoning my gaze
To her distant shore.
If she would raise her face

In the evening sky
And show herself bright as the moon
Burn away the steam
Of a long spring day
And hold me through the night
I would be comforted
By the peace of her embrace
Lifted heavenly by her beauty
And surrender finally
To her eyes upon me
I then catch the last glimmers
Of the day's light upon her lips
And hide the stealth of splashing
Until tomorrow's war

Stars

If I could make a million dreams upon the stars tonight
If I could tell the children of the world to pull them down
And hold them tight
Everyone has the same reach, look up and know I will be there
Every child knows ….I love them

If I could hang a thousand words on the stars beyond the moon
Keep them closer for everyone to see, so people would not be hurt
I'd tell everyone, " look, they're within your reach"
I'd ask them to hold onto them and bring them down
There are so many children to teach

Be not afraid
Be not afraid
I come from God
Be not afraid, don't be afraid
I am with you behind the same stars

If I could hang a loaf of bread or a morsel of some wheat
From every star above the constellations, as far as you could see
You could try real hard to fetch them down for yourself
Or would you look at the stars and pray you could give them
To someone else

Two children staring at the moon
Two children different in how their lives will move
One won't eat today, drink water, or even die soon
One smiles at the television devouring cheerios with a silver spoon

And I am here, behind the stars
I am watching you
Watching you
I am here in the oceans blue
I am here in the mountains
In the fields and the streams
Looking at what I had wanted it to mean

Don't let the light fade
Don't let the slim take them away
It's possible to reach to the stars
It's possible to do it right from where you are

Today, kneel and pray
Two children, different sides of the world
Two parents looking at boys and girls
One can provide, one might die
But their love is the same inside
Reach for the stars, you can do it from where you are

Pray today, "do all you can", I say
If you forgot I was around, you'd better check again
Because I'm right where you might not even look for me to be found
I'll be there again and again

Look for the star shine from the children's eyes
Look for the love deep, deep inside
Take the journey within
Know that we can begin to make a difference now
Look within, take the journey within
We can make it, we can make it anyhow
God's love will shine from the children's eyes
You can find my love there
Don't let one of them slip away from you
Don't ever forget life can be fair

I gave you everything you needed
Everything you needed
Everything you need

If I Am to Be a Flower

OK, I will look with favor upon myself
As not only just a flower
But a massive red rose
Seductive in my fragrance
Interesting in my movement
Dancing to the rhythms of this life
But grab hold of my stem to admire me
And my thorns will cut you like a knife

Rooted deep within timeless soil
I hold tight to this earth
Appearing sweet, shedding gentle petals
Yet catching up in your fabric and stabbing you
As you pass on the path

Beware the rose, the stately flower
For it may beg you into love to see
But beware the thorns and broken stems
Watch out for the sting of a hidden bee

No wonder I worry
That I will always be alone
For I often forget I'm only one
In a garden which brings beauty to this day
Thorns and sticks, fences and dirt
Lie behind the lure of the colorful flames
But without my horns, my ticks, fears and hurts
My rose would never grow
For only through the thicket
Will I ever truly know
I am one flower
I choose
The rose

Heaven's Heather

In a great tall window of this masterful place
Reflected back before grand oaks, I saw my father's face
And as I stared to hold his image inside
I saw his father and his father's father
And then began to cry
Through my weeping and my battle
With my own broken windows and shattered pain
I saw a steed stroll across a field through the window pane
Quiet through the shade of full, green, patient trees
And on into the sun-soaked heather rising to his knees
A peaceful stroll, a stare back, a bow
The stallion stands out in the herd.
Perhaps they have found their field and own their peace
New peace in a world just beyond the wall.
I am pressed to the cold pane in my window
And long to be with them someday in the sun
But for now to know they are strong where they are standing
For they have truly won
My life is rich and full and fun.
So I will only visit the window and gaze through its prisms
When life's colors are bending, not blending
And have me on the run.
There will be no regrets or disappointments through my days
I will mount up what's left of courage
And gallop through the morning haze into the sunlight of today
I know beyond the mysterious window a field awaits my feet
But for now I will canter through this mansion
In hopes of mistakes I won't repeat
There is so much time and yet I have only this day
To live, to love, to weather
"No worries my son" I heard through the window
"They'll be plenty of time in the heather"

I Am Your Affirmation

I am your affirmation
To know my love is to know
Life is worth an effort
To feel my love is to seize the words
Of hope, of heaven
I am your affirmation
Heaven, an oasis on the other side
Away from pain, regret, fear and anger
A meadow far from hunger, poverty and disease
A forest tall and protective
Long beyond the roads of lies
Betrayal, greed, slothfulness, gluttony and blame
I am your affirmation
It is not necessary to die or pass away, to know
I am your affirmation
For until you arrive
You are always invited
To peace, to love
I am your affirmation
For I am broken, lost and confused
And yet I am loved
For love is all that can be affirmed

Steps in Time

The Stain

Hang my weakness before the day
Hung from the windows of my eyes
They drip the guilt, embarrassment and shame
The blush and sour scent of my face paralyzed in pain
How many times must my life, my experience
Rake in a flutter in the wind
Across the rough siding of my withered walls
And flap, as if in an angry, sarcastic tone
And pound my world
Look! What are we to do with you?
You've done it again!
I want to crawl beneath the earth, a final stone
Far too many times I have walked this way
And there, down the road, a vision of my home
My heart sinks, my courage collapses
My mind overloaded and fear freezes my soul
As my blindness and blurred vision see ahead
Flailing from the window of the classic Cape Cod gable
All can tell, they see clearly what I struggle to believe
The urine-soaked linens fly from the sill
A yellow sun sags to grayed wet rims
And bold white ripples
In a springtime breeze, it slaps the wall
And my heart falls again
Then the thought that, three sheets to the wind
Is nothing compared to the pain of my one
I may never be able to trust home
I can smell fear down the road
It is my own

Wednesday

I breathe
That's all
Just breathe
I embrace my breath, feel, taste and sound
It drinks in the morning
And every inch of peace to be found
Slowly, yet in an instant
My body follows an awakening mind
I wade into the dawn
Like a bather immersing himself
In chilled North Atlantic waters
Easing this way and that
Stretching, lifting
Trying to be as small and sleek as possible
To sneak through, avoid the impact
Of the ever-rolling waves
Finally up to my waste
In the ocean of my awareness
I dive face first into the day
Now, if only I could learn
And find the courage to swim

Fall

Burn your stance upon me so golden
So browned from the teasing heat
Flames flicker as my face bursts ablush
Shed the vibrant, colorful garments
No time to trust
Heaped upon the floor
Scattered, restless, leaning into the skin
Beneath the weight of predictable tears
Then stand you all, tall
Nailed and naked on the branches
All before my frightened gaze
Beautiful, bony and masterfully mysterious
Your shadowy, whipped arms clasping
Colliding and reaching for wings
Asway in dizziness and shivers that look in horror
To each other's trembled descent
The gray, dark, sorrowful, weeping
Floods the sour sponge of earth below
As the thunderous claps of lightening
Sparks a slab of a random tomb
Taste the last breath of yesterday
Before climbing beneath the sheet's ruffled gust of virgin white
There quilted together, far below the cold drifts and drafts
Crowned and blinded by the bleeding ice
That tickles the silence and hails to the still ceiling of sparkles

That illuminates the deep blue evening's distance
And hollers the echoes of misplaced dreams
Hold tight in your starry stare, astorm with concentration
Feel the roll of anticipation
Aware now, of movement below
The pebbles of doubt tossed aside
The silence broken only by the sighs, wheezes, whistles and whispers
Of aromas cycling in the midst
Mysteries, deep, and down deeper still
Pulling covers, raps, upon covers over and over rhythmically
The heavy, heaving smoothes the vast horizons
Cloaking the valleys, hills and powerful plateaus
Run into hiding, penetrate the calm caverns, crevices, deserts bare
Walk across solid waters, mirroring the reaches of creation
Slide into to a comfortable embrace
The embers of a new morning
Peak through the crisp, waving blinds of the distance
The sweat begins to drip below the throws and pillows
Alive, one's glance devours your landscape
Catching the eyes of dawn that melt the soul
Press doubting fingers into the thick wounded bark
Know the scars have strengthened all
Flowers are abundantly presented by mother
Upon the grave of yesterday, at the birth of a new spring
So gently take me, own my reach
Heal my heart with color, with light
For you are my love......My Fall
May I sleep in your arms until Summer

Perish Not

Perish not
As your brief colorful life loosens and flutters
Like trembling hands of older, wiser folk
Your veins turning brown and hard
As they gray your frail body before the gust of cold to be
Afraid to let go of what could have, would have been
Might have, if only
Perish not
Perish not
Release your grip
And ride the wind for a while
Whip and spin for one grand, fast, vast view
Upon the brisk breeze
Make every effort to hold onto
The bark of a tree,
The steel of a fence,
The last blade of lawn
Like ideas, loves and dreams long since gone
Rest like a child making angels in the snow
Feed your fractured frame to the ground below
Send your spirit to the sky
Rest in the frozen stillness
The brilliant quiet
Perish not
Perish not
Die to life, to fly again
Wave on, reach for heaven
Fresh, hardy, pastel greens
Grace your smooth, shiny surface as you spring again
Maybe this time beyond your sleep
You're a mighty oak
Not a lonely maple leaf

Just Missing You

Missing you is an aching, gnawing pain
That reaches deep into the marrow of my bones
Like an old man's knees on a cold damp morning
I struggle to stand and not buckle beneath the weight of distance

Just beyond the walls of this my ancient architecture
Just out of my view and vibration of your sweet voice
To awaken my spirit
Is too far, too cruel for a heart weak and wearied by broken hope
The strain of the moments seems endless yet alive with possibilities

Missing you, I reach for a dream, a glance, a thought
Where are you now? Are you smiling and free or could it be
That somehow a thought touched in and our distance joined
For a moment, an instance, we were we again, and one

Just out of reach of your touch, is miles and continents away
Just inches away from your embrace leaves me out among the stars
Un-tethered to earth, left lost and wanting, determined to hold on
For there is more than your hands that reach for me

Missing you, I cup my hands to my face
To devour your taste that stays upon my cheek
I draw in a breath of your most holy scent like an anguished prayer
Of an old man that clutches the scarf
At the wake of his wife of fifty years
Knowing, death you can't have me yet, for youth
Has seized my dreams again

Just up the road, a stone's throw away from love
On the other side of today and singing in my tomorrows
I think of you again, your beautiful face gleaming in the cold winter sun
And I stand tall and strong and rejuvenated in the glory of your light

Missing you every minute and my heart screams with pain
That reaches deep into the marrow of my soul
Like a young man's gut after his first kiss on a warm summer's eve
I struggle to stand and not buckle, for I am willing to fall the distance

This Again

The nicks, cracks, clicks and knocks of walls and grout
The drips, splats, pops and taps of pipes that bang
Gusts outside, wind and rain
The tic, tic, tic and talks of the time clocks
Silence in pieces all about
The sip, sip, sip and slurp of a hot, strong brew
The morning is either coming apart at the seams
Or falling together, expanding and contracting new dreams
Is that my breath?
My choice, it's true

My Little Girl

Pink dress and parasol
Pigtails and paper dolls
Long walks with you on my shoulders
Watching you growing older

Jump rope and ice cream cones
Sunday church time, then time at home
Barbie's and mushy books
Content questions, how it looks

Silly stories and games of tea
Playground challenges
Sore, skinned knees
Bicycles and boys at school
Hugs and kisses
Goodnight I love you
Tears of joy and fears of pain
Funny faces, watching the rain

This is what you mean to me
Life and love she means to me
My little girl, my little girl

All the things you mean to me
You complete my dreams, you set me free
My little girl, my little girl

Tap shoe dancing, sing alongs
Shoe top waltzing and car ride songs
I'm just happy being in your world
Life's worth living with you, my little girl

Summer's Day

Weathered steel gray shingles
Fall out of quainter view
The warmth of wood and soaked pillars
Pales to the glare of midday sun
Heavy, humid heat
And the sounds of flip flop rubber
Slaps on a busy hectic street, shuffling feet
Colorful clothing drenched
Curvature of large and small
Men and women, teens and toddlers stroll
Short and tall, wide and thin
Coming out, squinting, ducking in
For a cooler breeze, a fan, some shade
To sing, to dance or thrill
There's too much fear about - Too much doubt
Cash is king but he's hiding out
In case of bad weather or overdrawn
From banks gone broke, from greed.
Gone wild now, everyone's like
A depressed 'wooden nickel child'
"Don't spend, just look"
Maybe ice cream to share
The tide is in kissing the pier
It will return again to the deep
Busy, busy Bear Skin Neck
Rich isn't enough
Wealth is not necessarily safe
It looks like a fantastic summer's day
But don't judge it by its face

Sunset – The Second Day

Orange, so much orange
Behind me a violet sky
Hovering over a steel blue sea
Pinks frame the horizon
Holding up the yellows over the Boston skyline
Tomorrow should be a fine day
All the lobstermen have returned to their moorings
Their dark silhouettes stern to port,
Bob easy in the Nahant harbor
The mild roar of jet liners
Approaching and leaving Logan
Hold the edge of the sky
The gulls begin their "goodnights" in the distance
Shrouds and staysails ring the dinner bell
Calling the tide in once more
I hope change never changes
I am constantly awed by it

Mask of Fear

Fear may obscure our view of a loving God,
Of a place of light
For fear casts a shadow
Across our path and slows the momentum
Of our inner light, desire, enthusiasm
Because it wields swords and weapons of painful lies before love
Fear breaks our view of the light but not our connection
Lectures should illuminate
What we already know to be true
In union with that which is Spirit, truth and vision
We are co-creators with God
We are powerful with God
We are allowed to be that voice
So speak…
Truth

There Was a Woman

There was a woman who changed my whole world
I never even met her or got to tell her she was right
But the message that she gave me that summer's afternoon
I think it really, yes, I know it really saved my life

I never got her number, I don't even know her name
I'm still so blown away since she said
"They're so glad that you came"
I'm going to call her Lily, for the place I found my heart
And that will be the start of this very special tale
About the beauty of Miss Lily Dale

I didn't go to Lily Dale to seek fortune or fame
Oh yes, I was curious, but I thought it was all a game
I wasn't expecting any miracles or blessings on that day
And God knows I didn't think I deserved one anyway

But in that tranquil forest on a quiet, peaceful afternoon
As I sat with so many others in a cathedral of nature's womb
I heard a voice calling and describing what I had on
And she asked if she could come to me
I said, "yes", though I was torn

She said someone on the other side had been waiting
Waiting for so very, very long
So listen and try to understand, they come to you in song

I never got her number, I don't even know her name
I'm still so blown away since she said
"They're so glad that you came"

She asked my name, so that she could hear my voice
This was not what I was thinking and certainly not my choice
She told me my dead granddad was standing by my side
But when she said my mother's name
And described her, I couldn't help but cry

Momma died when I was twelve and she was thirty-nine
It meant so much to me to know that she was doing just fine
And as she described her, my heart and soul became so free
And my mind began to open, as the message from Spirit lifted me

I never got her number, I don't even know her name
I'm still so blown away since she said
"They're so glad that you came"

My life had been filled with anger and self-torment for many years
No amount of pain could have been washed away by tears

I'm going to call her Lily for the place I found my heart
And that will be the finish of the very special tale
And of my new found love, old Miss Lily Dale

Please Help Me

Please help me, my everything, my master, and my peace
To lead my soul with grace
To honor my gift
Abundantly diverse and rich
Honor that which I am and are becoming
Please God, help me to define who I am
Not by where I have been
But by where I have not gone
And have yet to see

A Birthday Poem

It is another year behind
A new adventure just beyond
This mark, this day
The years don't come easy
Or roll in all at once
Every moment builds a day

The body once shiny and new
The mind once the sharpest knife
In the drawer it's true
Torn and tarnished, but no worse for wear
For the spirit's young

Always
Anew
Always
There

My day's wish for you
My awesome friend
Is to have love in your life
Joy in your heart
Every grace that God can bring
That the random homecoming
Reveals your happiness
So your
Soul
Will truly sing

I Love You More

I love you more
Than all the waves
On all the shores
In all the world
In all of time

I love you more
Than all the trees
That ever sprouted
On all the hills
And valleys
From Oak to Pine

I love you more
Than all the hardened stones
That crumbled to grains of sand
More than the dust
That lay behind them
Upon the land

I love you more
Than the wind
And drops of rain
From the beginning to the end
To where we go, from whence we came

As I preach my poem of love
It seems not nearly enough for you
You're every want, I ever wished
For all my dreams of life anew

The Empty Room

You may be gone
But not forgotten
You may be somewhere else
But I know you're still around
Your room is gone quiet
Yet I still hear you
Your chair may be empty all day long
But I still feel you and know you're not gone

Some try and console me
They tell me they're sorry
Yet I can't hear them through the tears I cry
So sad and so lonely
And so full of worry
Even though I know it's true
I know you did not die

There is no death, there are no dead
We do not die after this life we've lead
There is a more peaceful place
A heaven above
There is no death, or there is no love

Every day, every moment I think of you
And the memories we had
And I have my times when I don't know what to do
Because my heart hurts so bad

The littlest sound or a gentle breeze
A special song, a baby's sneeze
No matter how long my life will be
You live, and live well
In my heart you see

I don't have all the answers
I don't know how or why
And even through all the pain and tears
I know you did not die

There is no death, there are no dead
We do not die after this life we've lead
There is a more peaceful place, a heaven above
There is no death, or there is no love

A Heart's View

I Am Waiting for Your Call

Waiting for your call seems like a life sentence
Behind my own walls
The time creeps along at a snail's pace
And my frantic heart is poised like a tiger
Ready to lunge into the chase
Your soft, soothing voice is somewhere
Gently, peacefully calming someone else's ear
So I wait and wait again
For a buzz, a ring, a knock or a ding
Dawn has never seemed so long
My feelings stretch out
Across the landscape of morning
Like shadows from the rising star
I hold close to your center
And yet fan out in all directions
Defining your brilliance, framing your light
Praising your power and preparing your way

I am waiting for your call

Curb

I came across a man at the end of the road
Looks like he's down on his luck, don't you know
Some people will pass, strut right on fast, stay on out of his way
Some people ask him, "Bud, are you okay"?
Some people might even pick him up and put his head on the curb
Some people just walk the other way
Can't we see, there's a man on the street?
Can't you see the man on the street?
He's lying everywhere
Can't you see the man on the street?
He's right next to you, he's your brother
Can't you see the man so down?
He's lying down for you
You might say, "I don't care", easier to go along
"It's his problem, not mine"
Everything he does affects us all
Everything he does paints a sign
We're all crying

St. Patrick's

Somewhere between the doors of St. Patrick's and Saks Fifth Avenue
There is a story of love so painful you'll know it's true
With the cathedral full of towering concrete, spires and gold
I saw the starving village in my brother's eyes as they went cold
Elijah's wife's knees buckled at the sight of such a place
"So much, so much" I heard, from a hungry human voice
I told them if Jesus himself were to enter this place
He would tip the tables over in anger and shout out in mortal rage
I prayed hard but felt nothing but ashamed of all mankind
How could we have so much and leave so many children behind?
As we walked out the huge, heavy, ornate doors
It all weighed in harder as Elijah began to grin
We could feed a lot of people with the gold from just one door
Then my heart shuddered and my spirit dove beneath the floor
For right there before us at the curb of the street
An old man was picking through the garbage
For some waste that he could eat.
Far away in Elijah's village they have no trash can to find
And my spirit grabbed Elijah's hand as I screamed out,
"Has the world gone blind"?
Somewhere between St. Patrick's and Saks Fifth Avenue
Between glitzy windows and the grand mahogany pews
An angel rifled garbage to bring a story from above
The only thing that matters is my brother and his love

You Can Carry My Bloody Body

You can carry my bloody body across this hot sand
You can raise me up and wail at the top of your voice
In some foreign land
You can dream of days that will welcome better times
You can wash over letters that you wished you hadn't sent
It really doesn't matter to the Almighty what you've done
It's all about what you do
It's all about the message you send

You can lift my bleeding, broken body
Raise it up on high
You can wail and scream away your sadness
You can howl about what life has been
But here I am again.....here again

Every arm that drops
Every death, far too many and more
Every young man or woman
Who sacrificed for love in war
See it all
Can't you see it all?
Can't you all see that's all, no more?
I've asked you all to love
I've asked you to know what love can be
I've asked you carry the blood and body of love
Dying... for your peace

A Ministry Prayer

We will burst forth your light from our face
Lighting every soul we meet
Help us look through the cloudy bottle
Of the alcoholic
The cutting smoke of addiction
The grey darkness of age and loneliness
Look through the chaos of anger, crime and violence
Burst forth and expose the dim hope of the lost and poor
The shadow of death
Make our eyes your own, let us see
Close our eyes and pray
Dear Lord
From within our own darkness, help us find you
Shower us with your light of hope
Drench every corner of our hearts
With the crystal waters of your heaven
Bathe us in the sunshine of your peace
And drown us in the bright brilliance of your love
Help us Lord, to open our eyes
And look upon the ocean of tears
Help us see and reach out, to wipe away the fallen pain
Help us Lord, to walk toward the darkness
Bright, strong and true to your call
Guide us Lord, to hold our love tall
Please send us Lord, into the sea of despair
As your hands, your feet, your eyes
And let us not tire, weaken or waiver from love
For we are your ministers, servants of your truth
And all eyes
Are upon us

Somewhere

Somewhere in the middle of the world
There stands a little eight year old girl
She hears explosions in the wind
And there again in the street
She holds her ears and drowns in tears

Somewhere in the middle of the world
There is a boy of five in bed
He's shaking like a leaf
From the images in his head

Somewhere in the middle of the world
A mother collapses from the pain
The news of a dead son
Brings tears down like rain

O Lord God, Heavenly King
What will it take for peace?

"I will bring nothing
You were given all you need in the Lord"

"You have been given the weapon
To win every fight
You must search in your heart
And do what is right
You were given great wisdom from Spirit above
And you know how to use it, if only you Love"

"Love one another
As I have loved you
Do to others
As you would have done to you"

Buddha and Mohammed
Allah, Great Spirit and Christ
All had the weapons
And all sacrificed
It was never manufactured
Never feared or caused any pain
It was never created
Never held from any name
So search your hearts for truth
And pray to Spirit from above
And you will
Hear it
Mercy in the wind
An explosion of love

Eighteen

His mom – a call from Manhattan detention
Wrong place, wrong time
Good boy
It's a crime
Shot twice, one to the head
Eighteen, never nineteen
The boy's dead

Could've, should've, would've
Shot - that isn't nothing
Carry the pain, twist it and turn it
Take it on like you somehow earned it
"Where the hell is God in this"?
Locked up, shut up
Can't even give the boy a kiss

"Yes, I'm pissed, where's God in this"?
Shot for a second time
The pains in our heads
Complacent, blind, slothful
Self-centered time after time
Leave another mom lost, another boy dead
Shoot God, Shoot till you've got our attention

Life Is an Empty Sky

Lightning cracks and smacks across the clouds
Rain falls and slaps against my brow
And all was too quiet before the storm
Darkness creeps as daylight weeps
Thunder rumbles from behind the sheets
Of rain that drenches, the pain my bones have worn
Lord's fashion, your passion
Without them both, life is an empty sky
Rapids swell and rage below
Paths are blocked by the driven cold
And all was way too quiet before the storm
Flames collide and engulf the dark
Branches wilt and embrace the heat that chars the heart
That melts away the walls
My soul has born
Lord's fire, your desire
Without them both, it seems like an empty life

Dreams Afloat

Old Harbor

A tide of dreams
Glistens and pierces the soul
With sparks and shines of stones
Of hope, upliftment, gentleness
Blessings and bliss
There is love in this
Shanty shop by the sea
She brings a daring of more
A universal oneness
With peace emanating
From the flavors, odors and tastes
Of her core

From her mind to voice
To battle, to choice
She gives birth to her place, a soul
Love is the blessing
As lessons are learned
And growth unfolds
Love is the energy
That allows peace all around
Times may be tough
But she's the richest gal in town

A Man and His Dog

I happened upon a man on the beach with his dog
A masterful bull, looked to be training well
With a bounce and prance to its step
Long behind, there is a man who appears in his fifties
Fit as a fiddle, but grayed
They pass by swiftly, teasing the tongues of surf
That kiss along the sweep of waves
They retreat and fade to a distant speck
The size of two grains of sand in the wind
Beyond my holler or a scream
They blend with the browns, reds, tans, whites and grays
Of the distant fingers of earth, reaching into the sea, oceans away
I may never meet the healthy man
Or the playful canine
Yet the ocean will whisper wave to wave hellos
And now I miss them on my horizon
And I wonder
Should I get a dog?

The Ketch

The ketch drags it's dory
Like a baby elephant holds the tail of its mother in migration
As she reaches for open ocean
Before her, a rolling blue sea framed by stratus clouds
Rocky coast, sequins line its edge
Small, gentle waves slap against the beach and stones
As if applauding a classical music concert in final bow
Beautiful and sleek, she disappears
Behind moored sloops on the horizon
Gone from sight, to sea, forever in my memory
A picture at anchor in my soul

Good Morning Rockport

A lone cloud, adrift across a thick heavy fog
Begins to glow hot
Yellows, reds, and oranges
Like a toaster just beginning its time
The ambers catch the heels and feat
Of the wandering bed for dreams
The dense fog begins to run from a deathly gray
To hints of blues and reds
Each drumbeat of the crashing waves
Marches in what was tomorrow
And the gulls announce the screams and barks of excitement
The awakening of a mother's new hope for all to see
The rocks lay quiet
Like outstretched hands
Calming the tides
The sands now smooth
Rest with lines of offered treasures
And the sky lifts with each wash of foam
Cleansing with hope
For there is always tomorrow

Oooh That Smell

Nostrils flare and seize a moment
A slight sting deep between the eyes
Natural pungency lifts the senses
As a breeze raises the dried death
From the salty carcasses of low tide
Stones mortared in the damp sand
Catch the withered skeletons of flaky seaweed,
Rolled-over crabs and snails
On a string of dark, slick, dragon-like tails
A few fine selections of beach combs
Enrich the smell where fish once were
Now only to rake the thought of purer skins of coast line
Is the death scent a natural one,
One to rejoice of promised tides to be beached?
Or is this stench mixed with the shallow,
Greedy and pompous generations of rushed wants?
Is this odor the piercing, random, pustuled rashes
That will wash upon the reach
Of children's dreams yet to come to sea and see?
I just want to sit and see the sea,
Is that okay? Is that alright?
Wave us in, wind and earth
Help us, this crazy world
In the light of her sun,
To breathe

Ghost Ships

Ghost ships on the horizon, I know you don't believe it's true
Ghost ship on the horizon crossing over the furthest blue
And she is carrying my love
Steaming towards the edge of the world
I know I have seen it
Heard her wake splash the shore
Then it disappears again like all the dreams that I have endured

Ghost ship on the horizon, oh how peaceful she does move
Ghost ship a-glimmer, she keeps surviving
A misty morning, a hollow dew
And where it's going dreams can only dare
She's loaded down with quiet thoughts of morning
Staring from easy rocking chairs

Have you seen her? Don't let the music pass you by
She's out there on the horizon
Love knows we will all take the ride
We'll all take the ride

So sail beyond your horizon, love please don't disappear
Sail over your horizons and my love will follow you there

Tall ships, fishing boats and frigates stocked
Cast the line, dories full of stories
Leave your cargo on these docks
Pink sky at morning, sailors take warning
Red skies at night to their delight
Sailors let your hearts go soaring

So sail beyond your golden horizons
But love, don't ever disappear
Drift on over your horizons and my love will follow you there
My love will follow you there, follow you there, follow you there

Life of Celebration

Cradled in an aluminum cloud
Blanketed with mold and mildew, she musts
She must sit and peek out
At yet another passing Summer
Beside the prestigious lake
Massive as a great white whale,
She withers beneath the
Weight of time
Her skin buckles and wrinkles
With popping sores
Her bones brittle and dry
Her ribs swell of death
Soon to be exposed as they strain to breathe
Yet another day
In the seemingly final corner of life
Once the princess of these waters,
She floats only on memories of
Past presidents, celebrities, and
Stories of love.

A ghostly feel fills her hull
As objects mark times gone by.
They sit tired and lifeless in the
Shadows of her rotting innards
One can almost hear her weeping,
Begging for the end
As the monster heat and squatters
Slowly and painfully reach like
A cancer into her once youthful figure
And tear away at the muscle, nerves and skeleton.

Perfect mandala webs crafted by quick
Talented masters tether the corners
Throughout her frail frame
They glisten like rainbows

Fluid but taught
As they appear to drape the furnishings, guts of her bowels
And truss her span, holding her canvas high
Like a grand brimmed hat aloft
One flimsy gauze of silk lace all but collapses
Under the weight of stowaways
Apparently hitching a ride or trying to claim a berth.
She's held together now by an army of spiders,
Coagulated grease, layered bilge sludge
Sticky spills of fruity booze and ruthless rust
Rigor mortis befalls her chrome, latches,
Hinges and joints
Death can't be far

Some say she will never swim again
Others speak of past times,
Stories with final and distant dismissal endings
Others estimate her longevity
The potential for a rebound and the great cost
Of life again

Whatever her fate from here
Only time can reveal
For each day as her beakish bow points out
Toward the crow's foot lower reaches of Chautauqua Lake
One can almost hear the celebration
As she revs her huge diesels for a sail
For she is the princess
And although she be tower-bound
There is still the hope her prince be found

Shall we revel in her past adventures a while
Allow her to drift off to decay
Or will her prince arrive soon
To revive her from the poison
To celebration of new days

When my engines falter
And my hull droops toward ground
Will I be put away, forgotten
Alone just watching time
Or will the waters
Call me, float me
And lift me upward
To sail just one more time
For life's a celebration
Don't ever miss a day
Sail on
Even if only in a dream

Feelin' Lazy - Mark's Quest

The grand Silverton hull fills the rusting barn
Rising up the steel truss
To be covered with warbled, silver sheets
Bolted-on to block the tears of falling sky
Backed-up and cornered alone in the dimly lit shadows
Of the weathered hanger
Frightened and feeling it might never be the same
Might never see the daylight
Or feel the buoyant bounce of a brisk day
Of waking waves against its belly across old Chautauqua
Insides cut out, torn, left open
At times neglected, always left wondering if life will come again
Ripped out, rib to rib, bow to stern
Only to be strung back together, customized
Sewn back and rigged part by piece
A healing hero of a greater fleet
Made to work, to hold on
To live and breathe again the sweet smells of the marina
The barbeques and the stories of the next craft adrift
To hear the creaks and the slaps of staysails
And the grindings of old engines
Struggling to catch youth again
Some of her structure and skin
Are pulled and stretched to fit and function
Almost to look fast and fluid standing still
To appear quick and alert
To mask the dull pains of days gone by
To appear to leap forward even though she's held back by time
Healed and hailed for a comeback
For the strength and courage to dive again
Parts replaced, weary from the race
The heart is strong and stands firm in place
Questions are asked
"Will she ever be finished, will she ever be done?"
And like her captain's life, the answer is, "No"

She will embrace the lake again
She will taste the sweet breezes and swallow the sunsets
She'll skip the surface of Chautauqua
Like a child on a swift sled
She'll slide through winter
And shake loose the suffering of the past
She'll spring into summer to brighten the days
For all those who greet her
Like her Captain, she's a survivor
And although no one knows what time will bring
And sometimes the world looks hazy
The strength of spirit grows greater still
When we're simply Feelin' Lazy

The Miss Kitty Lou

A deep navy blue canvas
Full of pinholes to heaven
Frayed, worn seams across her ceiling
Slips behind the hint of a misty quiet dawn
Awash in pale hues of light
As reflections of sleepy, snuggling, spooning shorelines
Gently flicker and adjust upside down, stretching forward
Dilating across the glossy surface of this upstate teardrop
Which wells with emotion on the lower lid
Of Lucy's legendary place of birth

The strains of painful, creaking cries
Echo off the rippled face of weedy soup below
Stirring the weeping, squeaking,
Weathered wood of piloned docks
Ropes expand and contract
To cradle floaters on this eye of earth
Then there she sits before me
Strong, tall, awake behind the lifting morning fog
As friendly and generous as her faithful crew
She towers in her grace
My guard is weakened, my heart melted
By the waking roll of her stately pose
She is the flagship, the Rose of the dock
And as I make my way from ship to shore
Drenched in the morning dew
I think to myself, I have never known this kind of peace
For my all too often broken soul
This taste of freedom is oh so new
And a tear wells up and falls from my cheek
To the canvas top of my bleached white deck shoes
She sees it all quietly and with great class and charm
She smiles sweetly like those southern belles do
And I nod back with enormous, yet gentle appreciation
"Good morning maam," I release beneath my breath

"A very good day to you"

For every morning I am grateful
There is always something greater
Always reason to hope and dream it's true
So, "thank you," I say with reverence and respect
For the plant of new life in my heart
For there is something healing, something wonderful
To begin the day anew
Something grand about the morning vision
Of her floating like an angel
The beautiful, Miss Kitty Lou

My Pequod

A big sky blue traveler waits in the morning rain
Cradling a sleek, thirty-six foot cruiser
That looks like it's in a hurry standing still
Her shiny, navy blue hull ready to leap into the drink
Dragging her stark white crown with her
As if it were already pinned back by speed like a fifties flat-top hairdo
Others roped in their slips, like broncos rearing in the passing wakes
Of an inconsiderate cigarette smoking down the river
They look to want their turn, to bust out into summer
Several white fiberglass bows reflect off a still somewhat quiet surface
Pitted like a teen's acne skin by the morning rain
Like a row of sparkled lips, puckered and aching
To kiss the new hottie on spring break - oh, to be young again
Wanting everything to be clean, trim and tight
Untouched, untried, just all mine
I'll take my Pequod, Old girl that she is
Weathered, wrinkled with her signs of broken dreams
You see the stories in her faded glass, past triumphant mornings
On the river of dreams, across from the land-bound elders
Who stare from the bowery to midtown as if waiting
To see her parade her pretty lines before the sun-licked streams
Behind workhorse steel ferries, sewing up the rip of distance
Confusing the view of starts and stops of the heart beats of the city
I'll feel the wood all around my classic little Maine-built, lap-streaked,
sport fishing boat
I'll rise on the river - that littered and worn highway
Up to quieter reaches and seemingly wider, safer distances
From the crowds and confusions of love and youth

A Poem for Clear Sailing

The wind screams through the whipping stays of the mast
Like the screeches of children
Chasing about the yard on a cool spring day
Hollering for summer's pleasures and breezy fascinations
The taps and bangs of the main sheet cable
Keep an unceasingly steady rhythm
Like a child's tugs on the apron strings
Of a busy woman at the kitchen sink
"Mommy, mommy, mommy"
The beautiful old center-cockpit yacht cries out for attention,
For summer, for open waters
"Take me with you, I want to go, please daddy, please"
A child-like dreamer, she begs to catch a full gust in her sleeves and fly
Fly free and safe held by the hands of her guardians
To love, to sail, to drink in her lines, to pull her close and hold her tight
Smart to every luff, and aware of every drift,
She reaches for more and runs open to new horizons
Like a child's thirst for pink lemonade and a kiss of confidence,
Anxious for even more
For as you love, so are you loved, wanted and needed
To embrace Freedom
To ride the gales of God

The Mist on the Lake

Scratchy quacks pierce through the morning fog
And lay upon my mind
Like the mist, struggling to tear from the water of the passive lake
A small gull lifts easily and is winged high
From atop a mast of a still sleeping sloop
As if to either suggest my path
Or tease my struggle
Go ahead gull, adapt to the vast blues of morning
And reach to eclipse the rising sun
I am not far behind yet my wings are weary
And my frame heavy with regret
My heart beats for freedom
My mind will surely tear from the waters
Of past mistakes
A short lull lifts and easily sings my cry
From atop the mask of my still sleeping soul

Fat Bottom Girl

Sky blue fiberglass draped with varnished wood and chrome
Like a classic ham and cheese on white
Thick and meaty like a high-stuffed, fresh sandwich
She knows what you're thinking
You can't help but love her, want her
Or take her all in with your eyes
For old has charm
Wide can't be ignored
Ella Fitzgerald, Winona Judd, Aretha Franklin
R.E.S.P.E.C.T. a Sock-it-to-me feel at first sight
With her trim bright blue bonnet and her impressive beam
She anchors the marina to old Lake Chautauqua
Like a mansion owns the lawn
And stands wide and strong against the wakes
From much younger and active crafts
She sits like a jazz singer
And sings of days gone by
Still welcoming with her open back deck
She smiles like the receiving arms of a long-missed grandmother

You can't help but want to sit in her lap
And soak up the day
There is no boasting, lean or sleek, snazzy design
Humble as she rocks
She holds herself bold and beautiful
A strong and confident plus-size model on the runway of time
Questions of her rearing and demeanor
Are often heard in the sweet summer air
If only I could be more like her
That old Sea Ray cabin cruiser at the Celeron Dock
Quiet, revered, loved, pampered, respected
Bold, bulky but reserved
Perhaps my mind, though heavy as her hull with pain and emotion,
Would finally find a gentle patch of lily pads to float upon
And just drift through another lonely day
Or maybe there's something better
For my deep and broken heart out there
Comfortable, warm, cheery, loving
An oasis on the water to anchor my dream
A sexy Fat Bottom Girl

Forever Saturdays

Etheric-like mist
Blankets the glass-covered lake
Sleepy, breathing, dew-covered hulls
Pale, still and quiet
One early riser breaks a hole in the shiny surface
Below the shadowy cover of a grayed-out dock
Spooning and nestled around an old Chris Craft
Dippy bill busy and wings splash
As the adolescent Mallard readies
For a day of work and play
Hung-over fog of the new light sparkles
As the sun begins to grab surfaces
Along aluminum masts and chrome rails
Reflections blind the efforts of dawn
The transom of the classic, majestic Chris Craft
Appears behind the dream
Like smoke of morn
And reads in the new law, the new way
And invites my soul, so torn
"Forever Saturdays" it cries
Forever Saturdays
All summer long

Mighty Morning

Rise oh mighty morning
Define the graceful hills and valleys
A hot, large gum ball flames toward the quiet
The moist dew upon a drape of canvas melts to tears
Pink, subtle yet brilliant pops lick up across the flow of dawn
Staring me in the eye, captivating me to an altered stillness
I boil within to embrace the moment
Fire engulfs dreams as the near blinding, spinning, dizzying spot
Grabs all my senses and pulls me in
If I am not cautious of my place
I may fall through her surface and drown in sunken yesterdays
Mighty morning awakes across the Haverstraw Bay
And the colors of now dance in the day

Shore Thing

Foamy licks of seltzer-sounding tongues
Fluttering against salty flesh-colored smoothness
Followed by intricate patterns of lace overlapping
Sneaking out from beyond the dark cloak of evening
Teasing my senses with each step and long stride
Like a delicate, tasteful slip peeking out from below a riding skirt
Caught on the tight, sandy hosiery adorning a perfect thigh
As it is caught on my eye, heart, soul and rhythms
Pounding with every stride deeper toward my longing
Riding up closer to my stare
The dark navy blue garments ripple and buckle
To give an occasional glisten
Reflected from the movement of the moonlit pillows
Midnight exhaustion, rolling and tossing awake with excitement
Layers of fine silk slap in the wind
Along the distance of a festive wedding table
The heaving stone floor rising to shape the dance
And the waves of a summer's night reach from the infinite mysteries
That is my ocean just below my window on this rocky beach
Sleep and dream well, the tide is always with you

You Are My....

You Are My Butterfly

You are my butterfly
Colorful, graceful and free
You are my butterfly
Gentle and beautiful to me
Life's the flower you flutter to
Your colors pierce the breeze
Like the warmth of the sunlight
You embrace all of me
You are my butterfly
Always lightly winging through my mind
So patient with the wind, so safe, so kind
You are my butterfly
I only hope to share your garden
For together beauty is abundant
And alone my heart only hardens
Flutter to me my monarch, my tiny bird
Free me from my cocoon, myself absurd
Let me float in your flower
Let me fly in your many hues
Let me love your sun and moon
You are my butterfly
Dancing across the flower of spring
Laugh at my awkward flight, yet allow me to sing
Cherish the song of each real touch
Enfold me in your wings
Love is
Love will
Love might
For you are my butterfly
Forevermore tonight

You Are My Sunset

Sprawled across the hot steaming sands
Settling behind the bowing grasses of the dunes
Beckoning my stare from the edge of the earth

You are my sunset
Rich in the hues of love and gentleness
Spanning beyond the peripherals of my imagination
You capture me completely like a ship in a storm

You are my sunset
I am tossed about uncontrollably
Rhythmically thrown to the depths of the sea
And thrust to the highest sprays of the raging waves
I am worn weak in your wake

You are my sunset
Larger than life you fill the sky of my dreams
Stripping away the last layer of old gray clouds
You fall naked and brilliant into the evening

You are my sunset

You Are My Oasis

A hope of peace
Across the desert of my doubting heart
Life rich with color, bold to the abrasions
Of the sands of time
You are my oasis
Strong, surviving
You brave to stand alone
Yet you wait for me steady and true
Through all the storms that well up and roll across my mind
Your greenery, flagging the heavens and marking your reality
With a healing wake in the winds
You are my oasis
An Island of rest, a breath of calm, a shelter from the trudge
You rise up from the beaches of pain and death
And lift lives laid to waist
And you greet me with a breath of new youth,
Of love and refreshing truth
You are my oasis
Through the waves of heat
My journey burns your stance like a towering city of peace
Melting my heart and electrifying my horizon
To move my soul to stay, to come
You are my oasis
You are finally the one

You Are My Angel

I have hoped and longed for you to be real
All my life you have held me
Walked along beside me
Whispered in my heart
Left me blatant signs
You have lifted me when I cried
Stepped in and grabbed my attention
Caught me as I've fallen
Been tender when I was so hard
Been hard when I would not move
Thrown delays in my path
When I rushed too fast
Forced me down when my ego inflated
More than conscience, more than grace
You kept me alive when I should have been done
More than mystery, more than coincidence
You kept my wits in your pocket and tossed me a laugh
More than a gift, more than a spirit
You winged in from every angle
You shadow me with light
You must be real
Just the thought of you
A hope for love
A touch from the pearly door
I have longed for you all my life
Yet I've known you've been there all along
Through every night, every day
No matter what the reaches of my own pain
You have pushed and pulled

Prompted and tugged
Raised me up and pulled out the carpet
Made me rich and bankrupt my soul
You have loved me better than I
Birth till death
Until alive again
You will shove me toward the grave
Then entice me a carrot so it's dangled
I have heard your call, felt your voice,
Smelled your sweet sweat, tasted your breath
So dangle, spin, shift and trip
I cannot shake you or cast you aside
You hold me for life
The perfect bride
To my lost, you are my find
To my life, you are my compass
To my fears, you are my fault
To my heart, the rhythm
The best beat, palm to skin
You are the stars in the heaven and the oceans at my feet
So go on, ram me back, tackle me down
Throw me aloft, sink me to drowned
I give, Uncle, Uncle!
I am yours to push, to dangle
Yours to love as I am your love
For you are my guardian
You are my angel

You Are My Surf

You are my surf
Wild and furious, powerful, beauty in rage
Rampage of consistency upon my shore
You are my surf
Constantly reminding, pounding and persuasive
Pure pulse, raw rhythm, drowning, drumming
And the resounding sound of a snare's release
You are my surf
You tip your caps and curl your lips
Your lashes a spray from your winking eyes
You pour over me again and again
There is no time to drift or dream
I am captured by your music, your gaze, your reach
I am engulfed by your majesty, fortitude and depth
You are my surf
I want to splash into you and feel your weight toss me to the bed
I want to crash through you
And bury my head in the swell of your curls
Dance with your rainbows and sing with your roll
Scream at every break like a fan at a rock concert
You are my surf

In summer you cool my body
And tease my taste with your salty scent
In spring you quietly soak up the tears of rain
Shed from fear of pain, of colder times
You sip from the sweet roses peeking out from stone cliffs
You lift the feathered songs of morning gulls
You are my surf
As I embrace your vast horizons of wrinkles and ripples
And follow your gaze upon my soul
We find our fall and I dive my skin against your wet heaving swell
Trying to hold on, just one more swim in your squeeze
But alas, I am tossed like a weed
In a burst of foam upon the beach of my reality again
You are my surf
In winter you move like a heavy quilt
Puffed, patient, warming my core
Even through the bitter wind
You rise high and pull the cold down in,
Into the deep green you harbor the healing of a true endless heart
Loving never stops and is always awake, alive, aware and allowed
The winds, gales and hurricanes may trouble your source
But you continue to wave, to reach, to rise above the storm
You are my surf
Never stop, no matter how many times we break
We will surf the tides of time
You are my surf

You Are My Graveyard

You are my graveyard so quietly poised
A garden of stories etched in old stones
You are my graveyard heaving with life
Between sinking memories of this world's pain and strife
You are my graveyard crowded with death
So still in the morning dew
Nestled in the fog of heaven's breath
You are my graveyard, the markers of those passed
The keeper of grief and sorrow
Soaking up tears along your stony path
You are my graveyard worn, weathered and washed
With rains of tears that heaven's angels have shed
For they are filled with love, for life is never dead
You are my graveyard, so loud is your call
The one where families lay
Those who taught me
And molded my way to never ever look away
You are my graveyard, that reminds me to change
The ends are new beginnings, that love always remains
You are my graveyard
I kneel before you on the damp heather in prayer
And lay another wish upon the doorway
Between us, heaven and earth
Graveyard, oh graveyard you are my undying place
Some day the door will open at the end of my race
We will meet upon tomorrow
Upon the shadows of the stones
You are my graveyard
My door, my gate, I hear you chatting, laughing
And wince to my dance, as I search for my key
You are my graveyard and someday
God will open your door for me

You Are My Garden

You are the blossoms of early spring
Flowers and fragrance and bright colors you bring
You are the garden, you are the great gate
Nourishing seeds of love as you patiently wait

You take the heat and soak up the rising sun
Spreading the warmth of gentleness to everyone
You are the garden, you are the earth
The giver of life, the angel of birth

You harbor the young at every fall
Covering them with warm colored blankets at every call
You are the garden, you are the rock
The timeless spirit, the soul of the hawk

You brave long winters and swallow the frost
Protecting life's beauty at every cost
You are the garden, you are the fine fence
Abounding love and poised in strength

You provide through the seasons the highest breath of truth
Overcoming every storm with the sweet love of youth
You are the garden, love like no other
Illuminated by God and sent as mother

You Are My Morning

You are my morning
A crisp new day
The cool new light of dawn
Fresh sound of life in my heart

You are my sunrise
A warm fire within
Spilling over the landscape of my soul
Waves of color bursting on my shore

You are my waking moments
Come alive with joy, of more
Ringing true in my thoughts of love
A wash of beauty and echoes of peace

You are my morning
My crisp new day

You Are My Pillow

You are my pillow
An oasis from my day
A hiding place from trouble
A home somewhere far away
You are my pillow
Soft against my face
You soak up my fears and tears
And rescue me from the race
You are my pillow
My distant fluffy cloud
Where angels come to sing to me
And those I've lost
Step out from behind the shroud
You are my pillow
My favorite smell, touch and space
You hold me up, embrace my dreams
And kiss my lonely face
You are my pillow
There to swing into the fight
Feathers fly and fun remembered
Bringing the light of laughter in the night
You are my pillow
Through every turn and toss
You always let me have my way
You prop me up with you
I'm for once, the boss
You are my pillow
Adorning, dressing,
And sculpting the beauty of my bed
I can't wait to hold you
And pull you close to me
And lay down my head upon your breast
And finally drift off to sleep
For a long quiet rest

You Are My Pathway

You are my pathway, my road, my avenue
My highway to the alley through the street
Of past, present and to be
You are the byway, the fast lane, the freeway
You are the potholes, the rough pavement
And the faded broken lines, I've crossed too many times
You are the twists and turns
Embankments and the barriers of my mind
The slick and the stones
The grip and the grooves of rumble strips
And breakdowns, spinouts and flats
Thin construction lines and windy fat hills
Sunrise, sunsets
Road signs, sharp curves and road kill
Deer in the headlights
Possums, the smell of skunk
The angry sweep of the clock
The cross left by a drunk
You are my path, my road, my way
I'm driven to drive, to walk, to crawl
And to love you every inch of the day

You Are My Lake

You are my lake
Lying quietly before my eyes
Distant hills in amber light
Covered with the feathers of a budding spring plumage
Lining the edges of your drenched valley

You are my lake
Reflecting the light of a morning sky
Moving and wrinkling, wisping and swelling
With even a hint of summer's breath across your skin

You are my lake
Surrounded by the curls and dancing bounce
Of willows weeping in delight
Soaking up entire attention and becoming my far away stare

You are my lake
Coming alive to the moment
The song of swans
The slaps of ducks' bills
The ruffling of great wings of cranes and eagles
The honk of geese
The chirp of chickadees
The coos of doves
The sigh of loons
And the alerting howls of coyotes in the distance

You are my lake
Echoing the noise of love and nature's choir
I long to glide across your surface
Dive deep into you and swim gently to all your shores
Explore every inch of your view

You are my lake
Mysterious and wonderful

I long to dip my finger in your wetness
And ripple a wave across to all sides
My wish, to wade, to jump, to dive, into your deepest colors
And know you are my love, my bride

You are my lake
My mirror of heaven
My call to peace
I will stay and live before your view
You are my lake, and I will always love you

You Are My Daffodil

You are my daffodil
My very first flower of spring
Above reaching arms of green healing
Bringing back the color
After a long winter's chill
You grab my glance, my joy, my heart
You are my daffodil
Sweet you sit, delicate atop a sturdy stem
Reaching for the heavens
Along the road, in the garden
Before the window sill
You twinkle my day and pop a peek to tease
You are my daffodil
Flutter and shudder the frantic, spring breeze dance
Our time together is short in spring
Yet I will love you still
Who knows what the season may bring
I will follow my heart
And God's will for purpose, plans and courage
I won't finally rest until
You are my daffodil

You Are My Storm

You are my storm
I have no control over you
You roll in quickly and overwhelm my world
You are fiery and beautiful
Sometimes loud and unpredictable
You quietly sneak up on my senses
And wisp in like a swarm of gulls
Fluttering my insides and capturing all my attention
You rain down rhythm and beat upon my surface
With gentle pokes and prods
Smoothing my indifference
And splashing me awake to the moment
Thunder and lightening
You electrify my passion
And throw me out of control
Running in all directions to survive my own confusion
My blindness in the wind
My terror in my field of broken dreams
And lost loves
You overcast my sunny delusions
And cloud them over
With reality, now, and commitment

I reach for shelter in your arms
And give to your power
And yet I leap
For a funnel cloud to rise again
In the tosses and turns of my own ego

You are my storm
I have no control over you
Drench me until I am so heavy
With your wetness that I cannot move
Rake and ravage me
Blow me down so hard
That I finally remain still

You are my storm
I may plywood my doors and windows
I may crawl to my basement
I may drive for the distant hills
But you are my storm
Beautiful, exciting, powerful and awesome

You are my storm
Mine
And oh, how I love a good storm!

You Are My Newspaper

You are my newspaper
And your time draws near
Saved by your own efforts
To inform educate, report and repair
Times change, evolve, some grow, some decline
Fear spins like the news
While technology whines
You are my newspaper
My morning friend
My coffee companion
You, I defend
You are my newspaper
I trust the black and white
As I read between your lines
You're the genuine article, the real deal
In step with the times
Your bold and broad titles catch every eye
Wrapped in bundles on the sidewalk
Awaiting a passerby
You are my newspaper
Sometimes celebrating, sometimes laying blame
You're nestled upon my doorstep
But your lies are never the same
Some mornings you're in the garden again
Or strewn all about the lane
You are my fresh paper
Wrapped up and slipped inside a bag like bakery bread
I thank God for you no matter how you arrive
Each day I check the obituaries
So I know that I'm not dead
You are my newspaper
Your headlines of politics, war, fashion and sport
Your ads for every auto clown in town,
Your personals and daily court
Are the columns that hold up my heart

My fingers smudged by your cheap ink
You're my wall between the goings on
And the early A.M. rush
Where I can hide behind your leafs and folds
While others tell all to hurry up or to hush
You are my newspaper
My shield and my sword
My topic, my partner, my "Get through the day"
Now you're spewed about on-line
Are you really going away?
Will there be no more paper boys and girls
No more trucks or stands
No more extra packing materials
Or loggers on the land?
You are my newspaper
My voice of reason, my lively debate
The thought of your leaving is something I hate
Can't you see I love you, now things won't be the same
Whatever happened to real journalists
When did they become so lame?
You are my newspaper always
So don't let technology win
I will miss you hanging on my doorknob
Or blown about the streets in the wind
I'll miss the piles across the diner counters as I sob
I'll miss the comic strips, the funnies and pages of new jobs
I'll miss the mess along with the magazines
But you're becoming gibberish in pixels across little screens
My God, not the mags too!
It's too much rag for an old man's blues
You are my newspaper
Funky headlines with a twist
You're now at the flick of a button
Not held proudly between my fist

You Are My Snow

You are my snow
Light and sweet, sugary in a sweep
Like foam on morning coffee you drench me in heat
Wisping, turning, whipping, and plump
You cover me, blanket me
And make my heart jump

You are my snow
You're brilliant, you're ominous, you're overwhelming at times
In beauty and beastly breath of stinging gust

You are my snow
Masking my rust, my dirt
Giving purpose to my pain
My lonely day, you fall and fill
And drift and shape and morph together
Cold rain and my heart and passion can't escape

For you are my snow
To ski and sled, to make tunnels
Plow and bed, roll and throw
Toss and crush
Sweep, rake, shovel and brush

You are my snow
My crystal palace of peace
No school, no work, no function
Release
I'll light a fire for you and me
Curl up with a comforter and we can
Stare at each other through the frozen window
And marvel at God's gifts

You Are My Ocean

You are my ocean
A shimmering, glassy swell
Heaving and bursting upon my shore
Turbulent, gushing, foaming,
Smoothing my surface, penetrating my core

You are my ocean
A humorous sparkling array of light
Whispering, spraying, rippling over my fear
Tickling the air about, gleaming with delight
Holding me in your attentive tide, dreaming, wanting more

You are my ocean
Powerful, mysteriously deep
Vast and rhythmic, full of life
Storms of currents below your horizon
Furiously beautiful, passionate and sweet

You are my ocean
So in love with the sky
Boldly alive from sunrise to sunset
Quietly waking from dusk to dawn
Waltzing in the clouds, embracing across our distance
Wading in, caressing at my shore

You are my ocean
My heart swims with you forever more
You are my ocean, may I drown in your arms

You Are My First Bird of Morning

You are my first bird of morning, perched upon a branch outside
Beckoning through the window
To begin my day, to leave my fears behind

You are my first bird of morning
Before the green, sparkled dew of the fresh manicured lawn
Awakening my song, welcoming me to dawn
I wish I could climb between your feathers
As you rise for your flight
Soar into the morning, bid farewell to last night
Reach for the heavens and look back over the land
Work with the angels
And ask everyone to lend a hand
Welcome in the morning and cherish the day
Cherish each other
For it must be the only way

You are my first bird of the morning
Take me to your sky
Help me meet my hopes
Let my dream at last, finally fly
Bring me far above my troubles and my doubt
Let me see from above
Let go of fear and become a bird of love

You are my first bird of the morning
Thank you for your feathers and your wings
Now it is my turn to fly
For it is peace I must bring

After the Falls

Looking Back

You may carry my broken body
Solemn serenity or in song
You may pray for my spirit
At the sunset and dawn
You can protest my passing
And wield in the growing pain
But it won't change that I am gone
And the same, will bring the same

Your warring and your hatred
Your clamor for your land
Is all so painfully ridiculous
From the plane now on which I stand
Your fighting and your hunger
For righteousness and power
Your greed for position
And the terror hour by hour

From the place to which I passed to
It all seems so sad
That the Holy Name of Allah
Be abuse for so much bad
And you say you will make it right
That you will force the peace
In the name of our Creator
And a lost brother like me

But it won't change that I'm gone
And the same, will be the same
So you can grieve me below
Or burn my body above
But no one of you
Will ever find Peace
Without Love

View From Where-ever

Spirit who are you
Where are you, and why
There are so many questions
So many feelings
Lost in a wasteland of doubt
How am I to ever know?
They tell me leap, trust, give in, let go
Like they know
Who is kidding who
Right, wrong or true
I must know, so I let go
Spirit, I will meet you at the corner of the clouds
Somewhere east of the lake of dreams
At the base of the heavenly mountains
On a bench made of warm, ancient wood
We will watch the angels float by and listen to their choir sing
You and I spirit, amidst the mist of wonder
We speak a knowing not of words
We will breathe in the aromas
Of fresh flowers, wet forest and new life all about
We will rest for long moments
And bask in the luminary of a billion stars
Gentle is the touch of our etheric bodies
Shoulder pressed to shoulder
Strength in our gaze of possibilities
There before us, a world of music and dance
Celebration, the chance to hope
Cheers chime out, like bells on high
Ring, and bring on love
Those who are love, will shine all through each soul
Enlightening the truth of the purpose of all
Knowing, as we watch our prayers are heard
Each whisper, an enormous flash of change
All will know they require each other
Everyone will understand, they are one another

Crashes and clashes
Will become upliftment and encouragement
Anger and hate
Become patience and teaching
Power and prestige
Become humility and service to the whole
Pollution becomes the sweet air of new spring
The oceans become clear and brilliantly alive
The roar of God will be thunderous
Like a lion pleased at the sight of his oasis
Great rains will be witnessed
Washing away the tears of generations
Cleansing the universe of souls
So spirit, don't let me go
Press your shoulder to mine
Know where I am, know why I have come
I will answer all your questions spirit, for we shall see peace

One with Them

We must rise above the waves of hate,
Prejudice, violence and fear
We must ride out the wakes of crime,
Hunger and homelessness
We must break the swells of neglect, abuse, and addiction
We must sail bow first into a raging gale of pain and darkness
We must tack into the wind of poverty
And hurl our nets against the storm
For we are fishers of men and women
And one with them
The broken, the lost, the unborn
We must harvest our souls
Theirs and our own
We must all climb aboard
If we are to sail home
And if our catch is to be plenty we can all rejoice
But if it be few
Let it not be by choice
For the sea will calm at the end of our day
If we try to fish again and again
The wind will call us
To hear the depth of their wail
And the spray will drench us
With tears of the frail
Our ripple of hope will bring God's spirit across
The faces of the vast ocean lost
And in the quiet of God's breeze
With our spinnaker winged high,
God will bait our nets with abundant love
So children won't have to die

Palms

Palms were laid to welcome Him
His palms
Were pierced
For our sins
All that we have
All that we give
Are roads paved with palms
Given by Him
We are the welcome
Spreaders of palms
All of our gifts
All of our charms
Given with love
By His own palms
Open our eyes
Open our hearts
Pave the road
Gently and smart
Palms are laid to welcome Him
Like a carpet for a King
He arrives in everyone
Love is what He brings

Look for Him on the road
In everyone you meet
Spread your palms to welcome them
Bow before their feet
Rinse the dust of travel and time
Your palms will soothe their sores
Share the bread and cup of wine
So they need not wonder more
Raise your palms to the heavens
Raise your palms and sing
For you have welcomed
The lost and the broken
The poor and the least
And with your loving palms
You paved a road as priests

So raise your palms to heaven
Raise your palms and sing
He is raised again within you
You have welcomed home the King

The Infant

Through a cool night's breeze, a star shines
There's a young couple restless, awaiting a birth
They find a manger warmed by burrows
There He's born unto the earth

And the night's cool breeze does mellow
As the stars shine warm above
High and bright a light is cradled
Whispering "The baby I give you, is Love"

The infant cries out, loud, full of fear
Before a world filled with hate
The baby smiles and illuminates the darkness
As if to open heaven's gates

Through the cool night's breezes the stars beam
As the clouds waltz across a living sky
Bolder strokes of light or voices it seems
Sing of praise that the Savior's alive

And the night moves quiet beneath the stars
Only angels are heard to sing
The shepherds flock to His side, from near and far
For this day we are blessed with a King

If you wonder where the spirit has gone
Of that birth night so long ago
You will find it in an angel's song
And through the love you show

You will find it in the children's song
And in the stars that glow
And the stars will shine from the children's eyes
And the light will pierce your soul

The infant shouts aloud in distress
At a world filled of shallow souls
The baby smiles the smile of Christmas
As if to say, "Father wants you to love each other so"

As love came so very long ago
And set our souls so free
The angel's songs have whispered softly since
And the breeze has carried me

So if you hear the angel and see the light
I pray a child's smile gives you peace
May you never forget Christmas
Or the spirit of love, please

Come About

If I point to a star, reach for the edge of the horizon
And gaze back at the face of the moon
Will you hale a wave of greeting like the tossed branches
Of an ancient forest in a morning gale
Will you hunt me down in the lost darkness of misunderstanding
And pull me to your womb
If I plant my feet firm where I stand, reach for regrets of tomorrow
And turn my back against the earth
Will you haul me from my grieving
Like a child from the jaws of a dog gone mad
Will you hold me down beneath the water until my breath has seized
And the gates of hell seem glad
If I place myself far from hateful snares, grab for a truthful query
And look hard upon my soul
Will you hound my potential, gleaming
Until the dreams have time to grow
Will you hold me down until the shaking stops and until I finally know
If I plant my trust in the garden of love, reach for tomorrow's grace
And look your son straight in the face until I no longer run
Will you help me wave a greeting
Like a clue's final luff behind a full blown sail
Will you hand me down the silver cord
For "I have captured peace" will be my last wail

I Promise to Call

I have a friend who will break my bones
Every bone to be exact
All he needs is a call, twelve hours
Then I wait for the attack

Why would a friend be so willing to do such a thing
Bust bones, cripple, and maim
He has his reasons, well-intended
However brutal or strange

He promises surgical precision
In carrying out the deed
"There is no charge" he angrily boasts
He guarantees I'll barely bleed

He promises if I make the call
He'll be there without delay
The hospital bills and a few apologies
Will be all I have to pay

I asked him, "friend, why be so hard"?
"Don't you understand,
Haven't you ever felt or thought like this
Can't you see why I made this plan"?

Stopped cold in the middle of a breath
My friend burst out 'real talk'
Called the plan selfish, foolish
And frankly very warped

My friend vigorously demanded more
He spoke of treasures lost
You drop your plan and do what's right
You have no idea the cost

Some friends who love you get frustrated
They threaten to kill you if you fail
My friend's a little different, you see
Promising total traction without bail

My friend made me promise
To make the twelve hour call
I guess the Dr's dose of gut talk
Can be the greatest love of all

Things are much better now
Things are finally coming along
But if I ever decide on suicide
I'll be calling my brother Don

Life's A Cinch

I have lived many times, this time around
Each exhale a death, each breath, new life…Vita Nova
I sail forward on a sea of hope, slow in the fall of my seasoned life
The days and years seem quicker, shorter
And the moments tend to last eternally
As the fields of marvelous dreams grows more sparse on my scalp
And the dry, winter-white spikes dance over my brow
My sight and pace slow to a stroll, the long road now shorted by time
Seems cobbled and interesting, pitted and treacherously exciting
The path behind me is trampled
The walks I've laid my foothold upon have begun sprouting
New, sharpened blades begging to tickle the fancies and toe-holds
Of younger men who are perhaps in love with its virgin edges,
Its fossiled, muddied footprints, its residual spirit, its history
Or possibly enticed by the wonders of vast mountains
Crossed and challenged before
Or the far-reaching fields of sweet grains
And hidden stories of remembered youth
"A cinch by the inch, a trial by the mile" I heard so many times
Across the landscape of my numerous lives
Bounced painfully from my father's business voice, off my troubled soul
And only experienced through the miraculous gift of watching and
engaging
In the pace of pain, the surrender of sickness in the days of death
His life of bringing home the bacon, fortified by the heat of experience
He commanded his spirit
And scrambled for the egg of new birth and freedom
Glistening with thoughts of explosive fire
As I cry out in search of light, It is so, I am to die a bit with him
So I will have no hesitation, no dreamy, distant pauses
That miss the moment, this second, this reach
Awake and aware of now, right now, and all the gifts of love
Mindful I will be before I breathe again, before I take another step
Before I move but an inch

Holding On

Overcast skies
Grays and blues washing out the sunlight
The feel of rain
The threat of storm darkness lurks
Its time, unclear
Making the best of the day
Shadowed and slow
Overcast through the grays and blues
Washing out the fire
The feel of fear
And the threat of stillness and abandonment
Dark night, living the nightmares
Time and time again
Making the best effort at holding on
Shallow and slow
Holding through the weathered soul

Inspiration

Inspiration
Means nothing
Unless it is captured
And brought to view.

Inspiration
Is a flame sparked
In the dry recesses
Of the crowded rooms of our minds
To move us to action
To change
To clear out
And allow the breath of passion
To inhale truth's light.

Inspiration
Gives purpose to sleep, slothfulness
Darkness and despair
For light wants so deeply
To define life's distance, encouraging our dance

I Paused in the Silence

I paused in the silence
Behind the clatter of the stillness
Stung within by the cracking whip
Of the gust outside
Fearing the searing, popping, engulfing fire
Terrified by the cold, cutting wind
Blinded and frozen by the heat of change

Come hope, and cool my anger
Come love, and warm my pain
Come truth, and calm my storm
Bring choice and end my fear
Bring knowledge and open my mind
Bring wisdom and discern my purpose
Freeze my path
Burn my stance
Melt my view

I pause in the silence
Behind the clatter of the stillness
Stung all about by the cracking whip
Of the gust within
Feeling the pleasant pain of fire
Tantalized by the smooth, curling wind
Bursting and furious with the flame of challenge

The Other Side of Pain

If you could meet me on the other side of pain
You could awaken me like a spring rain
No matter what has happened to your soul
There is so much more you should know

If you could meet me on the other side of pain
You could complete me and paint me back to life again
I know somehow you can reach through
For on this side, there is only truth

If you'd could greet me on the other side of pain
If you pray and demand that I express myself again
I know what you've lost has hurt you very bad
If you scream for revenge then the darkness is glad

If only you could reach for me on the other side
I know I can help if you let me try again and again

There's so much more to reach for on the other side
There's so much more beyond the world we don't understand
There's so much more to teach you in your life
There's so much more, so let me help you stand

Could you meet me on the other side of your pain
Could you drench me like a pouring rain
Could you hold me, pray with me and take my hand

There's so much more on the other side
So much more beyond the wounds of love
So much more if you look deep inside
So much more, there's no need to hide from Spirit above
They're there for you, they're there for you to use
They're for your peace and solitude through life

Please meet me on the other side of pain
I know I can help if you pray with me again and again

Just a whisper or a thought of love
Just reach beyond the hurt and hail your voice
Just seek me on the other side of life, it's oh so near
Just beyond your fear, it's within your choice
Just insight of where you kneel
Justice of love to allow all to heal

Call beyond death
Call beyond pain
Call beyond the lies of darkness
Call out my name
Don't be afraid, I am with you always
Don't be afraid, I love you all, in all I say

There's so much more to life, every moment, every breath
There's so much more to live
There's so much more to reach for and gather before death
There's so much more to experience that heaven wants to give

Could you meet me in a dream on the other side of sorrow
Could you call me out by name and walk into your tomorrows
Could you love me on the other side of pain
Could you shower the world with grateful rain
Could you call out, shout out, sing out with a joyful heart

Whisper my name
And the names of those who have gone before
Whisper the name of the Lord
And open love's door

The Storm I Can't Seem to Hide From

A sunny day with an ominous feeling of doom
The blue skies across my view begin to haze
The temperature of my soul shifts and chills in the silence
Rumbles of distant unrest begin to surface noticeably upon my horizons
All too familiar sounds and signs of impending rain
Tears and certain pain
The leaves begin to wisp, shudder and shake, creating a hissing sound
Like a balloon leaking out its helium and sputtering
To get caught twisted among the branches of an impossible hemlock
It's heading for the ground
Dripping from the upper branches like paint from an abandoned canvas
The threads of the heart are torn and flail empty
Past fear, past puzzled, past the screams of desperation
And the internal yells, raging and cracking loud
Lightening across weighty, white and darker clouds
Spun into the storm of delusion, drudgery and self-hate
Straight through to the fire on the lower side of the gates
Reach and hold on, surrender ego
No place to hide, grab truth and let go
Breathe and scream
Bloody red slapped against the gesso
The bristles of sable bend and ride the trail
Of beauty's path back,
Thrust into a salty splash of heavy, green waves
Pounding the shore of my run
Slowing me in the soft sands of memory
Tugging at the ankles of my tired defeats
Smoothing the dunes of righteous religiosity
And swiping the surface of my sculpture
With form, depth, light and life
Paint me as pain of buried fears in the sunset sky of forever
Mold my steel and hammer my marble to submission
So I stand strong to weather
Tall and confident at the central square of my love

To Breathe Again

To breathe again after the stifling, stiffness, constraints
And weight of heavy air all around
To walk out of my own fears of ignorance, arrogance and intolerance
Spread so callously aloud
The death of kindness and compassion lost behind a sharkskin shroud
The challenge is not to suffer the suffocating coughs and cackles
Of greed and envy
Nor to choke on the slothful heavings of a thousand runaway fears
The challenge is to change
Let time devour old trophies and reach the authentic taste of winnings
To release the world of rings and bobbles, suits and Windsor knots
To let a higher place take hold of you and train your frozen heart
To see color and symbols of truth beyond squandering and souvenirs
To be willing to open up a winning mind, to meet peace and quiet
within
To breathe again
To step outside the race and win all by being still
By living what's next and right and surrendering to heaven's will

Lost Confidence

I lost my life today
No, not like a hero in the sands
Flesh against a virtually invisible barrage of thrusted steel
No not like an elderly woman shedding a lifetime of hard jobs
And children gone amok
No, not like the withered warrior
Who battled the clock in some factory for forty-seven years,
Only to tire, retire and die
No, not like many
Today, I lost my courage to Trust

Attica

You men on the inside
We've shared a flask somewhere, a story or two
You men on the inside
Behind the mask of fear and cool
I've been inside this place before
I dare not claim it as my own
I've walked on paths all too familiar
The paths you men walked alone
I can only imagine the clock on the wall
And how it shouts from its mortared heights
Nightmares of the second hand held back by a call
And the urge for out, for day, for flight
Surreal but too real, I canter to the bellows
Down deep inside the tomb of fallen fellows
Hardened by each frozen gate
Slamming steel, jarring loose my spared fate
Angry cold stairs along this seemingly endless ascension
Worries for all who cry in the night
For what's been done has been done and it goes unmentioned
In this dark place, only truth sheds light
You men are many who share this tomb
You men are few who share these rooms
Men live on the inside
The weak run outside and hide
I never knew who I was or where I belonged
But I know now, you men upon this concrete sod
You men of this hell who now seek God
You men, humans, who hold down time
You men locked away for the greater crime
You men I see in the mirror face to face
You men without hope locked in self-delusion and hate
You men have taught me
It's time to break out of this place

Love Sings

Believe It or Not

I met a woman some time ago
She worked at a church I know
But to my curiosity and inquiry
She served good, not God
Reality not religion
Rights and decency, not rule and dogma or doctrine
Others might rear their skulls
Judge her and condemn her soul
Barrage her with passages and verse
To an exhausting droll
Or parade her faults through coffee klatches
With berating words and curse
If only they could step back a bit, just for a little while
Cease their anger, pity and posturing
And greet her day with a smile
She might tell them loud and clear
Of her faith in all that's good
Without the words of prayer or spouts of angels floating near
She'd express no belief in a holy God or religion
Or dreams like Hollywood
Rather she would display her innate kindness,
Love and compassion where she stood
She would show that she's responsible for all she says and does
Then she'd be seen respecting nature and life because she is REAL
love
There really is no need to fear those who deny the ancient passages
For it's in the hearts of all who wander through this life of challenges
In them, you hear the word of the divine seed
In those like her, in their intent and deeds.
So before you judge, take a moment and stop
For God's in all of us.......believe it or not

Do You Hear?

There's a volcano in the jungle
Lava shooting everywhere
Do you hear the explosion in the distance
Did you know it was the angel's tears
They have been watching you treating each other unkind
They've been shouting love
But you have been deaf, dumb and blind
Did you hear the explosion in the distance
Like a nuclear bomb hitting the village
On a Sunday afternoon
Did you hear the explosion in the distance
Did you know it was the angels falling to the ground,
For the sadness all around
They've been praying
They've been trying to step in and tell you why
But you're not listening
You're just rushing around making other reasons to die
Turn on your PC and your TV
Find a way to run
Because I know you hear the explosions in the distance
You just don't understand which one
Do you hear it now
Do you hear the explosion in the distance
Do you hear the shrapnel fly
Fly through the sky
Do you hear the explosion in the distance
Well all that is, is angels
As thousands of them cry
They're shouting out
Please…choose Love
They're dancing up a storm to get you to see
They're crying out
Oh please…choose love
Can't you see we need each other to be free
Can you hear the explosion in the distance

Like planes hitting towers hard, bursting into flames
Can you hear the explosion in the distance
Can't you see that it's the angels
Trying to save your sacred hearts
They're shouting out
"Please love one another's souls, you're not meant to be apart,
The world was meant for love
It's just what we want you to know"
They're shouting in the distance
They're shouting up right into your ear
They're shouting out love
With love there's never any fear
Can't you hear the explosion in the distance
It's like a tsunami hitting the shore
Washing thousands away
Can you hear them
Angels whispering
Have you heard
Are you listening to what they have to say
Listen with every explosion of your heart
Listen….No sound…
Love

Spun Round and Down – A Song for Don and His Brother

You walked beside a stranger when
You were both just children
You became friends long before
You knew what brotherhood stood for
Side by upside down
You laughed and cried, you hit the town
Your means, your dreams and holidays
Spun round and down
Spun round and down

A bond of love, a gift of fear
This happens sometimes when two grow so near
From boys to men
It seemed forever then
Joys gone so fast
Past the last
To start again

Once men, your paths drifted away
You were both looking for better days
Then you only crossed on holidays
Spun round and down
Spun round and down
Round and down

And off again on your own
Another face, a distant home
A lifestyle each chose
And on those roads, the mysteries rose
Puzzled by the choice the other makes
Repeated what-ifs as you lie awake
The silent thunder has rocked your heart
To think two brothers have to part
Gone forever at so young
Seems so far away

A distant star, but who's to say
He'll be there again on holidays
Spun round and down

At first, pain is a numbing ache
Tears and anger help pass the day
But what you don't know will sink in soon
It takes no magic or bright full moon
You see, your friend, brother, the boy you knew
Has left his path but now he walks again with you
He's there to keep you and loved ones strong
To tell a joke of a time that's gone
To advise and be advised
All that's good stays inside
Only good stays around
He'll come around
He's here to stay through holidays
Spun round and down

Busy as life may become
He's there as never there before
You speak and hear an echo roar
To let you know he's loving you
Closer than you ever knew
So walk again
But now, side by side and all around
You'll laugh, you'll cry, you'll hit the town
Your means, your dreams and holidays
Spin round and down and round again

Song of New Light

Sing a song of new light
Life beyond the Stars
Sing a song of new light
Spirit travels so far
Sing a song of a new world
A world without the fear
Sing a song of freedom
Spirit will come so near

Voice a song of new life
A world of compassion and love
Shout a song of God's light
Illuminate the truth above

Every time I see the stars
I hear angels start to sing
Sing a song of a new world
Where peace will finally reign

Gentle whispers, prayers of healing
Let the songs of peace begin
Hold me in your loving feeling
There is no more pain or sin

We are all here for the learning
To share each other's heart
We are here to teach each other
That's where the new songs start

So sing the songs of new creation
A world filled with grace
So sing the songs of all the nations
A whole new human race

Oh Daddy

Oh daddy, I won't blame myself
Oh daddy, I can't be that wrong
It's been so long, long enough
Oh daddy, been so much pain
Oh daddy, tears falling like rain.
My son doesn't need that
I'm not going to pass it on no more

Different world now, daddy
It's a world of peace
Different world now, daddy
It's a world of hope
It's a new world of peace, a new song

A world of compassion and peace
Looking out for one another, yes it can be
No more judgment, hate will disappear
Hey, daddy that's the only world that makes sense to me

So won't you pray daddy
For all the young men and women
That they don't have to fight
For the intolerable power of a few

Pray daddy that they fight no more
Pray for a world with no need for war
That they can love each day
To see it's the only way
A world of peace
A world of love
A world of hope
I can hear you now from above
Brand new day of peace and tolerance

All this for a new world to come
Finally the way
Of all there is to come
It's the world I want to leave for my son
So much understanding between everyone
So put down the gun
Pull down the gate
Throw down the chains of intolerance and hate
Put down the blame, it's not the message I gave
It's all about love, not war

So daddy, I know that it all sounds like a sweet dream
Yes daddy, I know, it doesn't sound like anything we could bring
But we're being helped all the time
To stop the pain, end the crime
Stop all the pain and so much more
Stop, just stop, and end the war

City Morning

City morning
Takes a little longer for the sun to rise
Above night's shade
Tall 'scrapers leak light slowly
To the bus stop corners
Where the old man waits

Newspapers are tossed out on the curb
Tied in a bundle to do a day's work
Bring 'em the news, the ones with coffee and the ones with booze
And let 'em know what the day will bring

Then count your change and climb aboard
It's another city morning ride
A car screams by
The sirens, they cry, cry, cry
The fear will open up your eyes

City morning,
City morning, once again

City morning,
City morning, once again

City morning
The old men watch the children
As the day begins again.
Politics are talked about
Dreams are tossed about
But no one really wants to bend

Last night's sounds are seen scattered on the ground
The storekeeper sweeps them to the street
Sweep away the wraps,
The sticky gum and bottle caps
The city wakes and hasn't time to waste

Then count your dreams
And climb aboard
Another city morning ride
We'll all get by
Though some are hurt and some are high
But please just don't turn your eyes

City morning
City morning, takes a little longer
For the sun to rise, above night's shade

There's A Place

There's a place where God abides
God, help us to be strong and find your light
And remain still in your incredible light
Like a forest of the tallest trees
Help us reach your light, won't you please
Like the mountains heaving from the ground
Give us vision to see over valleys and all around

Like a wave-lined shore that embraces the sea
Help us stand strong, won't you please
Like the ocean embraces an entire world
Help us breathe new life to every boy and girl

Like a desert warm and wide as it can be
Help us make the stride for everyone to be free
Would you hold the earth in the palm of your heart
And show us the way we can start

Would you give us the truth from on high above
Would you finally teach us how to love
You have come here with words of life
And yet the world remains in strife

I don't want to see the world lose
Could you inspire me to make them all choose
Could you show the words and visions bright
That will lead them through this dark night

What's your love for
What's your love for
Could we find a way…away from war

What's your love say
What's your love say
Could you find a way to a new day

What's your love stand for
What's your love stand for
Could you help us find a better plan to endure

I hate to complain lord
It's gone on way too long
Would you help us now, to be strong
Would you help us now, to be strong

Race with the Reaper – A Poem for Leo

Racing ghost, projecting cold white sheets, steel bed
Gray days, insanity, dark fluorescent, shuddering hallways
He fearfully imagines what might become
Of the man he knew when young

Puzzled, lost, confused, determined
Nightmares of nightmares and frozen pain
He doesn't know the extent
He wonders, does he still know the man

Bracing, steadying
Wife, family, strangers to the man
Digging-in for the long haul
He prays and prays again
Angry then grateful, then again and again

Limbering limbs in place
Standing behind the frequented warm, white entry
Steel sky, bright day, summer-sweet air sachets
He anxiously awaits a man and a woman
He knew when he was young

Hopeful, confident, strategic gambling
Worries of worries, terribly tame
He doesn't know the depth
But reads the distant faces through the window

Breaking, staggering
Man, wife and kids vaguely familiar
Crashing in from a long hall
He prays and prays again, sorrowful then grateful
Then again, then again

Sprinting against the gun
Perched upon a thin white rope, steel intent
First days, dark, tenuous, bellowing hearts
He probes what might become of them
And the man among them

Determined, faithful
Compassionately companioned, strengthened
Days into days, exhausted ear, patience is weighed
He knows the baton's been passed
He must run cool to win

Steady strides, positive, gentle boost
Light seen down the dark, long hall
He praises and praises again
Concerned then grateful, then again, then again

Elbowing evils aside, crossing curved white lines
Steel courage, glorious days, shadows fall behind
The inside track clears away, he sees what might become
Of a man he knows is still young

Positioned, poised, cautious, focused
Hopes of hopes and mended wounds
He clasps the medal of himself
He's encouraged by the metal of the man

Braving, supporting
Wives, families, strangers to the man
Dashing for the long hall
He praises and praises again, blessing them
Graced by them again, then again

Relaxed, back stretched, pacing through, tasting the finish
Cold white winters, steel triumph, logging the days
Sudden death, back at the blocks, the reaper's held at bay
He knows what can become of a man

Who knows his day is young

Patient, peaceful, alert and alive
Dreams of dreams and friendship reigns
He doesn't know the next heat to weather
He wonders, does the man

Winning, gracing, loves, passions
Strangers to struggles, illuminating the vast, long hall
He prays and prays again
Thanked then thanked, then again, then again

Racing life, the baton is passed again
Gleaming white light, steel truth
Better days, grateful for the start, fire away
The man he knew when young
Stumbles then flies, he sighs, he knows he's won

Posting, pointing, cheering, coaching
Wins of wins and new foundations
He's challenged the hearts, he's reconditioned a soul

Beating, trouncing fears, guilts and strangers to truth
He's shown the way through the dark long hall
He paved and paved again, a track for a friend
Then again, then again

To him - my coach, my captain, my friend
Thanks then thanks again, then again
All my heart and gratitude
My brother, my friend
Who knew me when I was young
Who coached me to race the race
And never more, to run

The Sun She Speaks

Will I ever find you
Will you know who I am
Can I trust in the darkened shadows
Of the seasons of this plan
Could ya tell me, could ya hold me
Could ya see me through
Could ya guide me, could ya teach me
Could ya reach my inner truth
Will ya tell me if I've fallen
Will ya release me if I fly
Will ya love me while I'm living
Ya know they say we never die

Can ya greet me, can ya meet me
Can ya touch the other side
Can ya be there for me baby
You know the sun she speaks no lies

Take me by the soul
And drag me across your storm
Torch my heart through your coals
And push my mind until it's worn
Give me air, give me sky
Give me your holy breath
Find me here, beside you bleeding
Feeding from your sacred breast

Grace me with believers
Your holy ghost will swarm
Throw down your silver cord
The contract has been sworn

I am your servant, I am your friend
I am yours forever more
I am your heart, I am your soul
I am your very core
So can ya be there for me baby
The Father speaks in rhymes
The moon is rising, mother earth is trembling
For the one who speaks no lies

I'm So Blessed to Be Your Father

When I was a boy I stood quiet at the end of a hospital bed
And watched my daddy put his ear to his daddy's, as the old man said
"I'm so blessed to be your father
I'm so blessed to be your dad
I'm so blessed to be your father
Through the good time and the bad"

Many years later with a family of my own
I got the call from my momma sayin' "honey please get home"
When I arrived I saw him there and he was almost gone
I sat and held his hand into the early dawn
He woke just for a moment and spoke not for very long
And as I propped up his head, this is what he said

"I'm so blessed to be your father
I'm so blessed to be your dad
I'm so blessed to be your father
Through the good times and the bad"

A few years later when I was on the road on tour
I got the call that rocked my soul to its very core
Some drunken fool had crashed into my son
On his way home from school
When I arrived at the emergency room and hurried to his side
This is what he said to me as I kneeled beside his bed and cried
He said

"I'm so blessed that you're my father
I'm so blessed that you're my dad
I'm so blessed that you're my father
Through the good times and the bad"

Many years later with my hair turned winter white
I woke with a pain in my chest in the middle of the night
But somehow I had the feeling that it would be alright
As I began to drift into the most incredible white light
In the light I saw my grandpa, my daddy and my son stand
And as they moved slowly aside I felt someone else
Gently take my hand
And say

"I'm so blessed to be your father
I'm so blessed to be your dad
I'm so blessed to be your father
Through the good times and the Sad"

Well I Don't Recommend It at All

When people do this or that
And it just ain't what you feel
You can go on listening to their epitaph
While your heart really knows the deal

Well I don't recommend it at all
No, I don't recommend it at all

When they go on telling you, you must stay the course
Or you'll have to finally conform
Your dreams are waiting and you are hesitating
You stay confused and so torn
Well they'll promise you the world with a pretty face
They'll make you wish you were them
They'll promise you their bobbles, leather and lace
And spank the life out of you again

Well I don't recommend it at all
No, I don't recommend it at all

They'll define your God for you and make you fear
They'll rope you in by the neck of a tree
Screaming verse by verse in a tangled snare
No man, no woman, no mouse, just sheep

Well I don't recommend it at all
No, I don't recommend it at all

She will hold you in her trance and say you're cool
Your longing for real love will leave you blind
You can't see the motives and intentions, fool
The lonely pain is your only sign

They will tell you, you are bad
That your views are sin
Then they'll march you off to fight
Support the troops and the government
Cause we are the only ones that are right
Well I don't recommend it at all
No, I don't recommend it at all

It's all way too much you say, I just can't go on
And you'll want to end it all
Why would you want to hurt someone you don't even know
So inside yourself you crawl
Well I don't recommend it at all
No, I don't recommend it at all

You gotta stand up, stand up tall
No matter how bad it gets, it ain't over yet
So I can't recommend it at all
No, I can't recommend it at all

Tickles and Tastes

Runaway Feathers

Pillow, my dear pillow
I don't mean to get on your case
But I've tossed and turned
Looked up and down
And I keep finding you all over the place
You're at my heels, between the sheets
On the floor or under the bed
Behind the night stand
Tucked hiding behind the blanket
By the wall
Here and there and everywhere
Once practically in the hall
Pillow, my dear pillow
Neither one of us has gotten sleep
There's no more time before morning
For me to change your linen
Or to count a single sheep
Pillow, my friendly pillow
Let's give up the chase and make a deal
You settle quiet beneath my cheek
I promise no more garlic
With my meals

Fathers

Tall, short, fat, skinny
There, not there
Businessmen, care-givers, doctors, mechanics
Barbers, factory workers, pilots
Bankers, thugs and criminals
Gamblers, alcoholics, preachers
Pushers, committee leaders
Straight, gay, loyal
Not so loyal

Loud, quiet
Sports enthusiasts, book bound
Attentive, recluse
Happy, funny, angry, sad

Good as gold
Downright bad

Fathers all and many more, I'm told
Still called DAD
Young, loving, passed, or old
Fathers

Morning Smoke

While most drool a last few
Attempts to maneuver
The outcome of a dream
As their bunched-up, wrinkled
Pillow cases and blankets show signs of stress
And the sun has yet to show strength
Against the long night's chill
An old woman fumbles through her shoulder bag
Sounding the shuffle of the stone
On the walkway framed in daffodils
Still pale against the purple sky
She reaches and prods and probes the old purse
And it looks like she is wrestling
A wild possum to the seat
Of the damp teak bench
Finally victorious, her lips moistened
She fishes out a fine catch
A long, slim, sleek cigarette
And with the skill of a Vegas magician
She spins it in her fingers
And plops it on her lower lip
The wrinkles behind the pale mustache
Bleached to camouflaged her dry, aged skin
Spike outward as her upper, floppy lip
Clamps down on her morning fix
A quick light tactfully executed against a possible gust
She puffs deep
Her body seizes
And behind a huge cloud
Of exhaled smoke
She looks up as if she's being watched

Don't Be Afraid of Me

Don't be afraid of me
I am only here to love you
Don't be afraid of we
We will shed the light on the truth
When we are alone at night
Spirit will embrace our love
Go gently into the white light
Peace in your heart my gentle dove
I know it's true
I will be there with you
We know the cord is strong
We both know that we belong
When I touch you there
And whisper you my songs
There is nothing more to fear
With love comes a whole new dawn
Don't be afraid of me
I am with you always
Be not afraid of Me
For I am that I am

The Shine of New Life

The lake shines
Like the steel red of a fifty-five Jag
Polished and buffed to a gleam
Forced to squint
In order to discern
Where my ride ends
And the new road begins
For This
My sunset journey

Ever So Gently

Ever so gently, summoned at all points of my being
Drawn down a beautiful, lush path
Carpeted with floating drips of nature's autumn glint
Like rose petals tossed enthusiastically
Upon the white runner of a cathedral wedding
They pave a soft, beckoning road of wonder and mystery
A step to step, pause and step rhythm
As my feet crush the damp mat of life and my toes curl in my boots
Pretending to quiet the thrust
Like an ancient native hunter on the prowl
From toe to arch, then a roll of the heel
The ninja-type movement overtakes my body
And entertains my moment
I am now keenly aware of every smell, every crack of a stick,
Buzz of a bug, whistle of a spirit-like wind
Slow to each taste of my senses
I am but waltzing with the giants lining the isle
My elders strong, draped in robes of oranges, reds, yellows
And royal maroons over their long, gray and varied brown tunics,
Witness my wedding to the day
They tower above me and nod their heads approvingly
Whisking me ever further up the road
Young and old, they dance to a melody of rhythmic slaps,
Smacks and fluttering reeds
A celebration for the quiet hunter who seeks only
To bag one smaller bit of nourishment of soul
The great trophies lie plentiful and hidden
In the brush of my opportunities
Up ahead beyond the flowers, lining the stroll
Between the pews of a forest of onlookers
Is a clearing, an opening or altered space rich in its thickness
A thousand vibrations of tantalizing electrocutions
Jolt me to the reception of enthusiastic relations
Stunned as I take aim at the beast of fear
And no less shocked as I let go my arrows of prayer

I toast the well-wishers who gather in the spirit
Of love and understanding
Drink to the truth echoed brilliantly off the arched ceiling
Of this basilica's sky
Flanked by the soldiers, healing uniforms of evergreen
A voice, all encompassing, sweeps me off my plane
As a herd of angels delivers the ultimate inquiry
"Do you believe, O you great and mighty hunter of love"?
Fear thrashes away through the thorny distance
And my answer rides the wind of my most holy breath....
"I do"

Christmas

Will you be there this Christmas
Will you share the holidays with me
Will you sit with me by the fireside
And watch the lights twinkle on the tree
Will you be there for Christmas
Can we reminisce and raise the cheer
Can we listen to the carols of yesteryear
Will we ring in the New Year
Will you hold me once again and tell me of your dreams
Will you share the spirit of a whole new world
That is brought by the life of the little King
Will you be there close to my heart
Wrapping packages of hope
Will you celebrate the love we share
Teaching everyone to cope
This is Christmas a gift beyond compare
This Christmas I am so happy you are here
This Christmas I bring you joy and hope and love
For all the world's tears this is Christmas
And I have shared with you and will be there with you for many years

Stuck on a Train

Stuck on a train to London
Stuck on a train to London
Power failure, been over an hour
No signs of relief
Train is packed solid, we have no seat
Surprising patience by everyone
"I guess this happens often", some man says
Soul train
Silence turns to chatter
Moans to laughter mark the time
Restless shuffling from car to car
The coach will have to wait
A splintered old man, his branches reaching for heaven
Collapses across the wires
And cuts the track's spark of life
On the half-ten to Liverpool street
Standing in mourning of this day's death
Upon the morning train, soaked by December's rain
Hours pass and then a sign
Chatter splits the quiet
In two to twenty minutes we'll move again
A temporary leap of faith
To the next station up ahead
From there, a bus or taxi or such
We'll pass the funeral of the old man
And be back on the rails to London again

The Cups

Drink in the ceramic sculpture
Cleanse the pallet of your thoughts
A surface full of old cups
Hanging from hooks on a brightly painted
Worn and weathered wooden wall
They texture the silent coffee shop kitchen
As they hover above the cold tile floor
Clustered, random, yet orderly, not placed by size or stature
Some burst glossy and loud
Some wordy
Others quaint, quiet, if not pretty and passive.
A few battered mugs chipped to the bone
Reach to hang on, hang on
Holding on
Just waiting
Admired, maybe, yet perhaps unnoticed
Longing to be useful
To be filled up
Held, embraced
Kissed by lips smeared with sunset colors
Warming the outstretched hands of earthier, frozen fears
Collecting long awaited rains, tears
Ahh… dripping, spilled like guts
If only they could talk
The adventure heard through the spoons
Stirred gently through their core
The sweetness of some sugary overindulgence
The curdling of some old, milky mother's ideas
Creamy clouds of youthful ideals
Make mine black, strong, and straight up
I'll take nothing
Large, small, tall, double shot
A medium to another world
If only they could sing
Of the clinks and crashes of so many truths

Secretly whispered and sung over their hardened brims
Abundance on the wall
Plots and plans, dreams and pains
Washed away a cup at a time
I wonder if this texture, this array
Is a reflection of my soul.
Hope my handle, my grip, remains wide and strong
For my cup runneth over
With life
With "Let me warm that up for you"

Lady Bug

A lady bug walks across the chair top
Towards the window and the afternoon sun
Casting a shadow of the travel behind
Long and larger than his own life span
Miles above the floor, light years to the door
A spotted, hard-shelled spec
Asking nothing but perhaps to fly
Like our own lives
Heading for the light
Leaving trails behind
Shadows of ourselves
As we race across time
A space in the universe
Miles to endure
Light years yet to explore
I walk with my lady bug friend
Across a quiet moment
Miles from my busy life
Asking nothing but to rest
Light years from my strife
I walk across the chair top
Toward the sun and open sky
And cherish a moment's journey
With life before
I die

Epilogue

Gratitude overwhelms my thoughts when reviewing this collection of work. For in the verities of these pieces, some simply apparent and others labored, like our life's experience, we encounter the challenges of our struggle to know our purpose, our influence, our reach and relationship to all. We find we are never alone, nor do we ever live inaccessible, or ever unloved by others who have lived, are living or will be born to this life's experience.

My prayer for you would be to honor your life fully and to cherish the holiness of your spirit!

My song for you would be a symphony of joy, a swing tune of dance, a rock song of drive, a country song of stories, a ballad of strength, a folk tune of sincerity, a rap song of awareness, a jingle of attention, a round of laughter, a hymn of praise, a gospel of emotion and a melody of peace.

My poem for you would be simple.

Roses are in fact sometimes red. The ocean is sometimes quite blue, but no matter what the world may do, I will always in fact love you. I will always love you no matter what you might choose!

I've assembled these writings with a little something for everyone who walks the beaches and breathes the breaths of life in time and for those who wander occasionally through different paths along the reaches of the edge of this, our wild wilderness.

May you be blessed and receive like Moses, walk like Christ, sit like Buddha, endure like Gandhi, give like Mother Theresa and may Allah encourage you to never waste an opportunity to honor all life and love one another completely!

Joseph P. Shiel III

CPSIA information can be obtained
at www.ICGtesting.com
Printed in the USA
EDOW031436020713
2112ED